I0722071

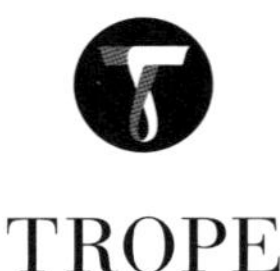

TROPE

TROPE PUBLISHING Co.

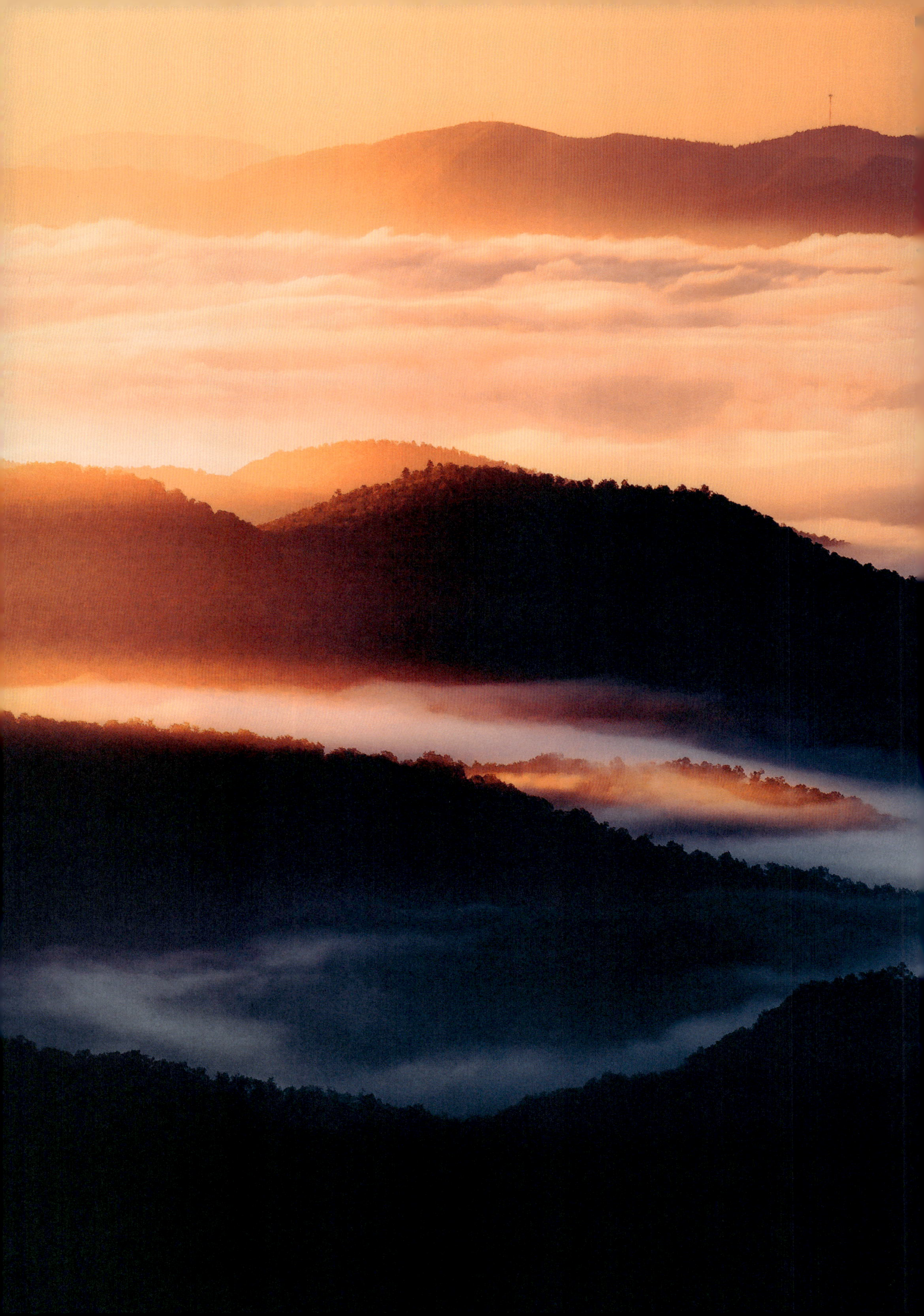

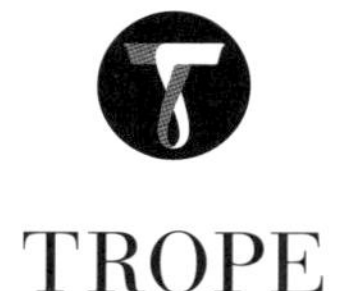

TROPE

BLUE RIDGE DREAMING

MIKE POGGIOLI

TROPE PUBLISHING Co.

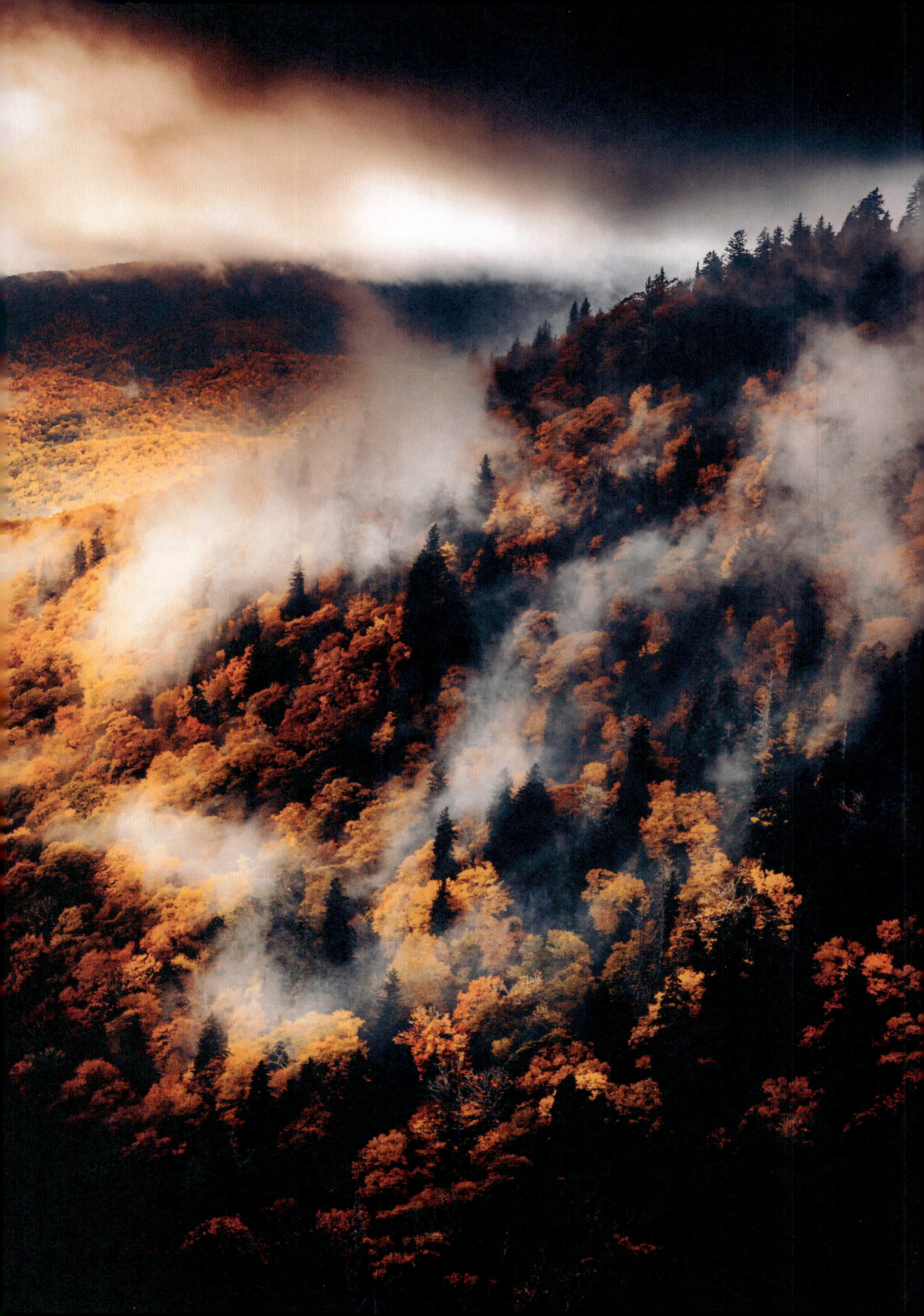

As a part of the Appalachian Mountains, the Blue Ridge Mountains begin in southern Pennsylvania and extend southwest, touching portions of seven additional states, including Maryland, West Virginia, Virginia, North Carolina, South Carolina, Tennessee, and Georgia. They are over one billion years old, making them the second oldest mountain range in the world, and at one point were among the highest mountain ranges worldwide. Millions of years of erosion have whittled the Blue Ridge Mountains down to be no taller than 6,684 feet, but they remain grand and majestic, always invoking a sense of calm when I visit.

I've spent much of my life living in urban centers, and in 2019 moved to Asheville, North Carolina. I immediately fell in love with the area and found myself driving again and again down the winding Blue Ridge Parkway at sunrise. It's such a dreamy experience: the creamy cloud inversions; the swirls of pink, purple, and golden light; and the stacks of wavy ridges that I never seem to tire of. The parkway offers so many different perspectives of these ancient ridges that there seems to be a new composition to capture around every bend. The photos in *Blue Ridge Dreaming* depict my attempt to capture the never-ending layers of the Appalachian Mountains.

Ansel Adams once said, "A great photograph is one that fully expresses what one feels, in the deepest sense, about what is being photographed." When I go out to photograph in these mountains, I feel truly at peace, immersed in their timeless natural beauty. I hope *Blue Ridge Dreaming* brings some of that same feeling to you – however far you may be from the mountains.

MIKE POGGIOLI
@mpthecomebackid

It is impossible for
the emotions arising
from the sublime
to be felt beyond
what they are here…
The rapture of the
spectator is really
indescribable.

THOMAS JEFFERSON

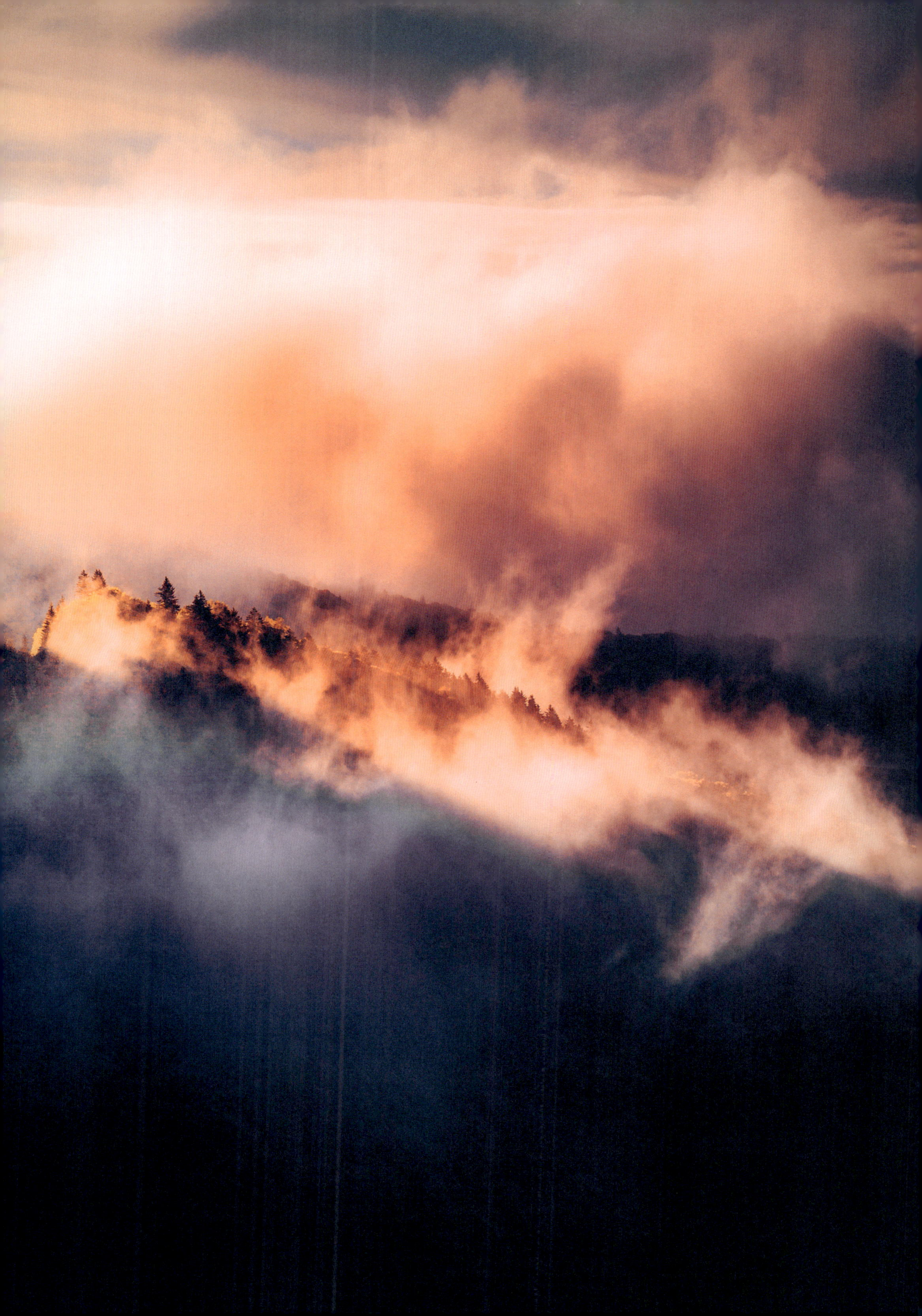

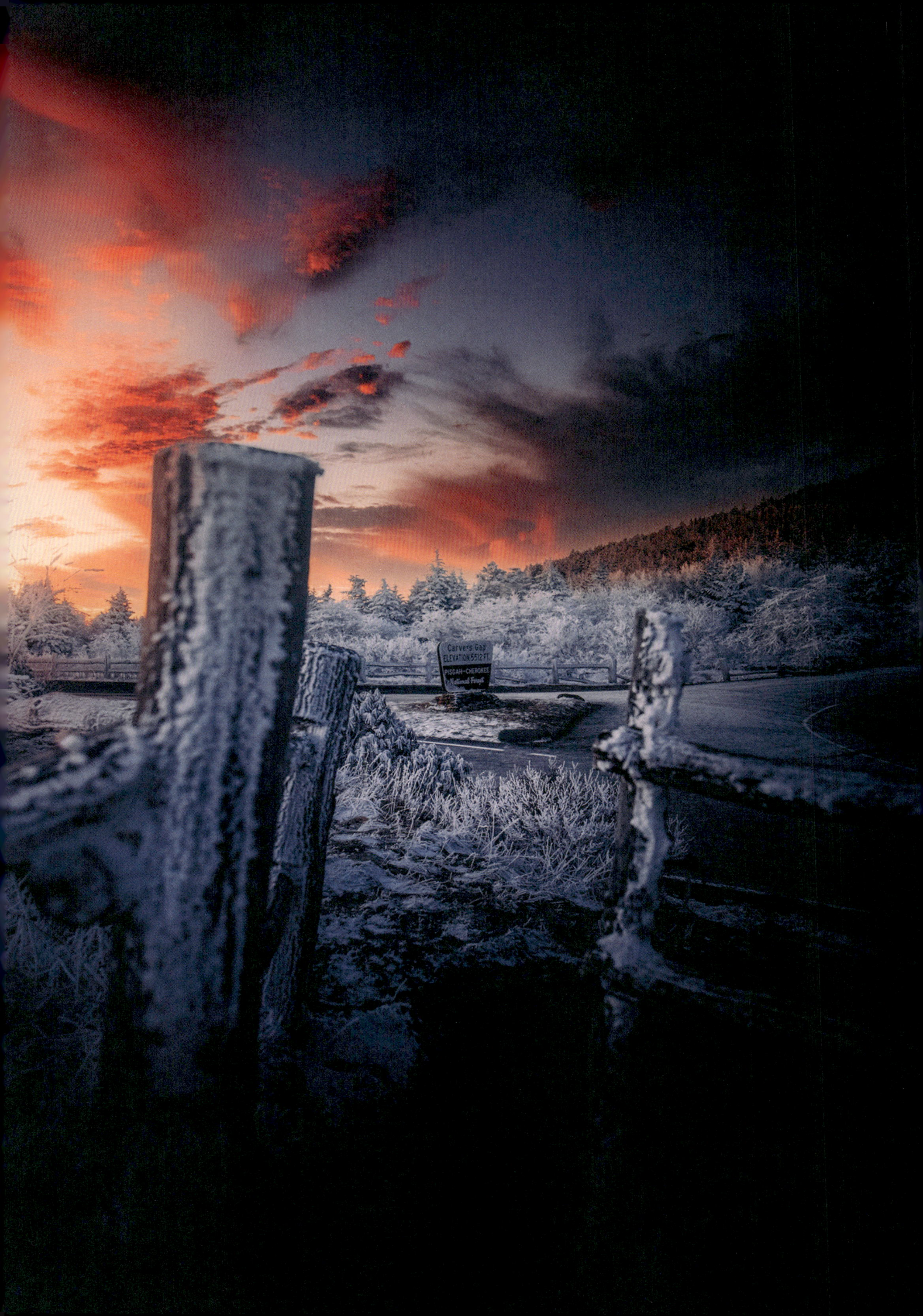
Carvers Gap
ELEVATION 5512 FT.
PISGAH-CHEROKEE
National Forest

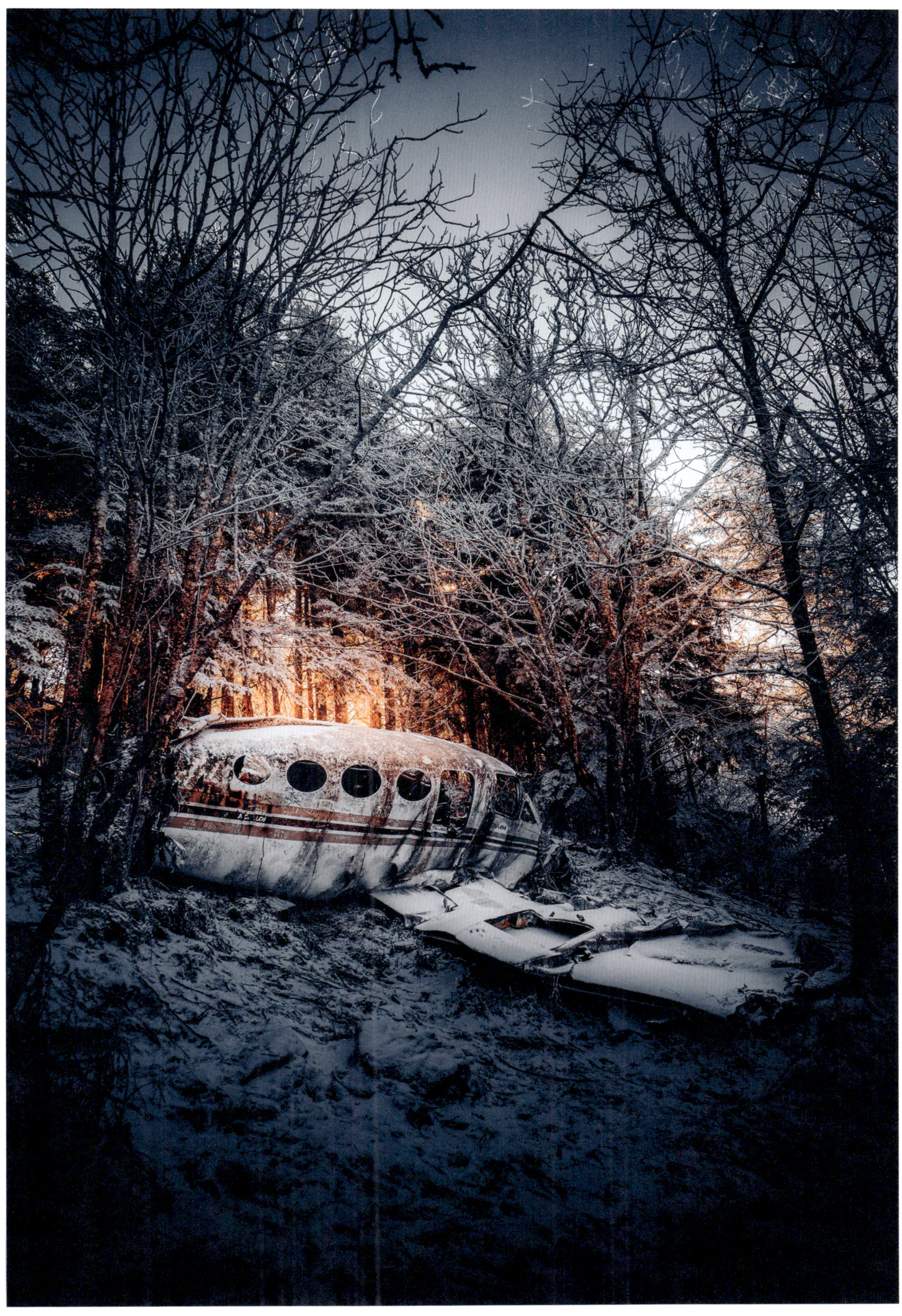

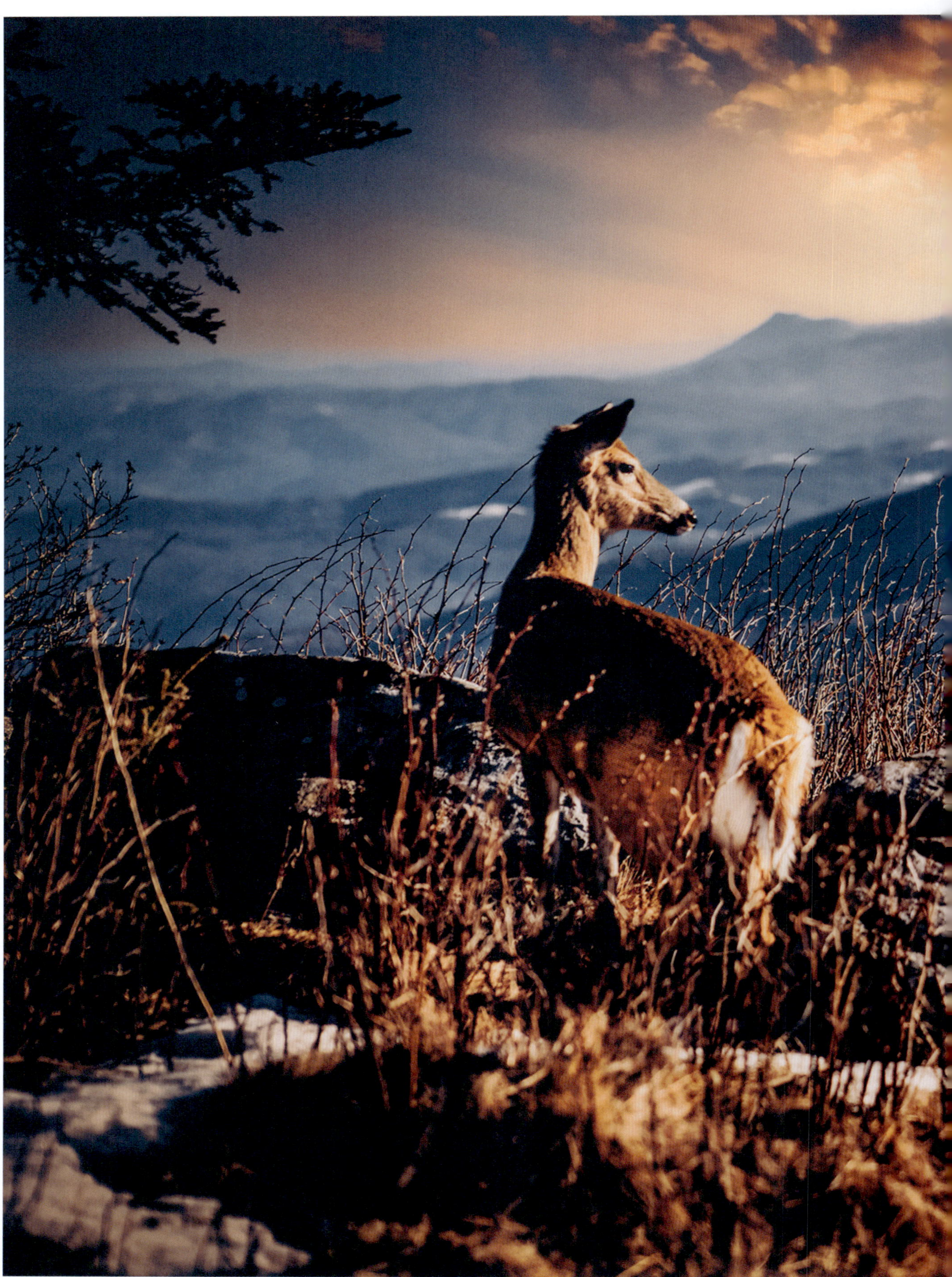

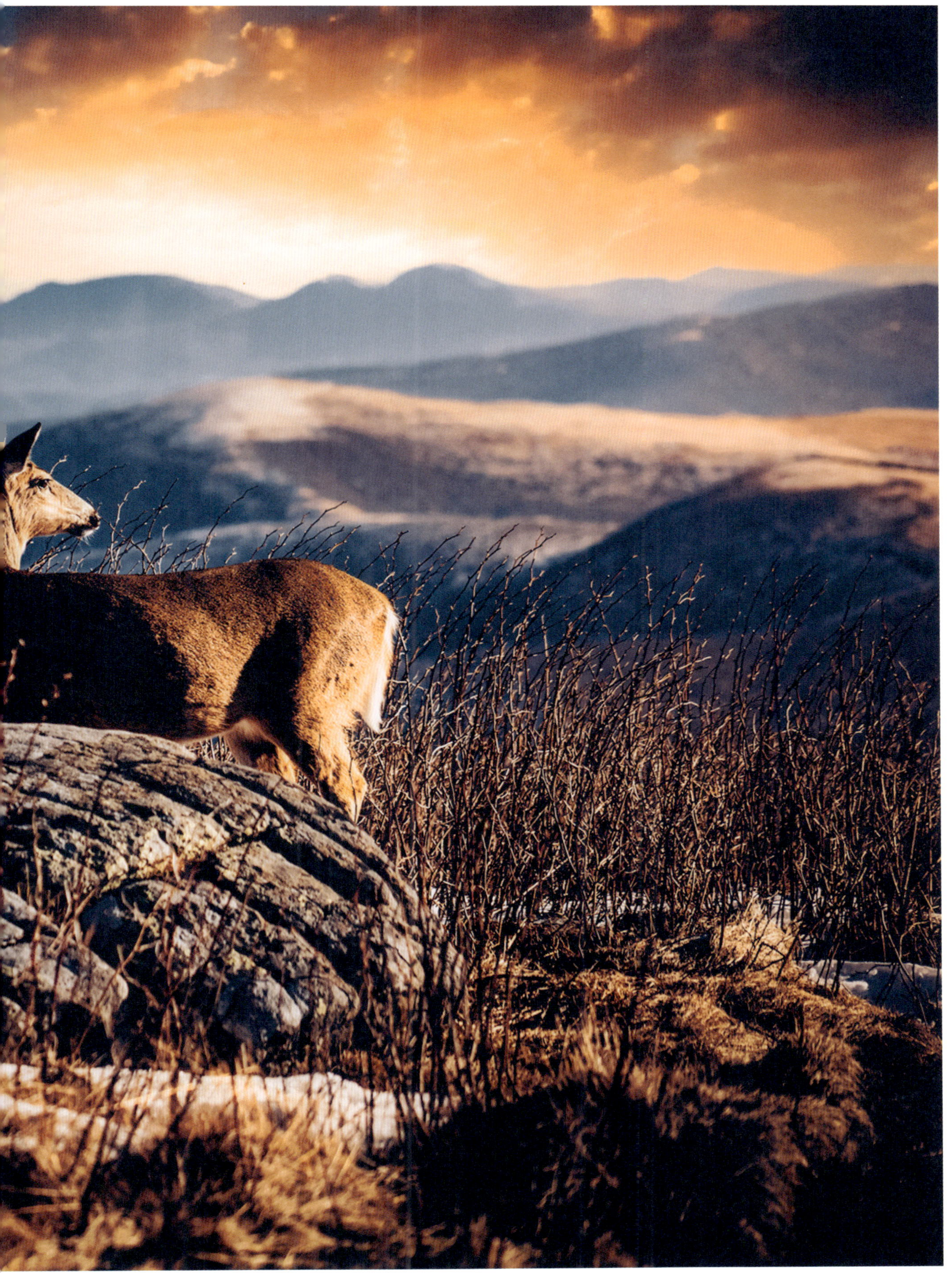

There is something
infinitely healing
in the repeated
refrains of nature –
the assurance that
dawn comes after
night, and spring
after winter.

RACHEL CARSON

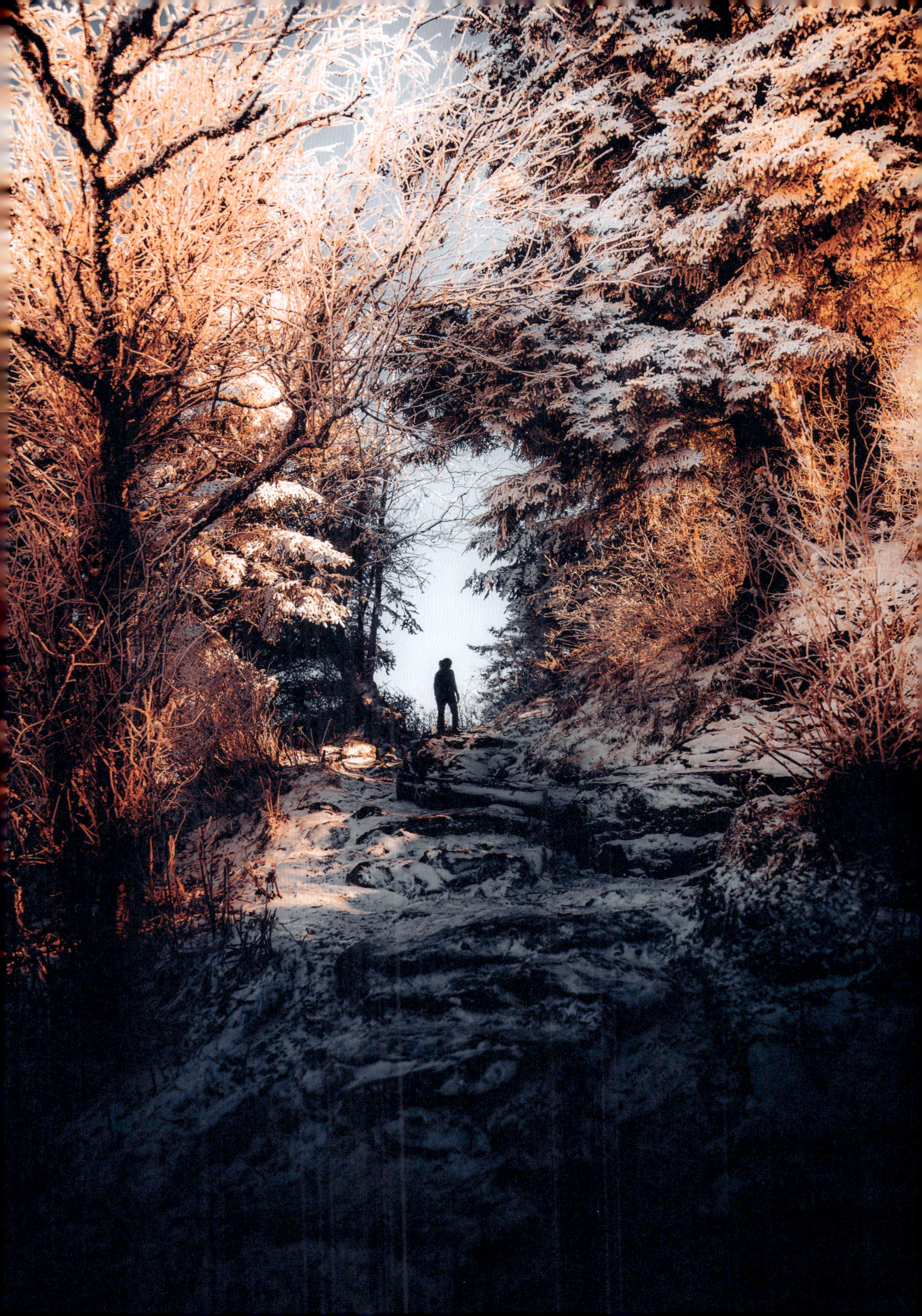

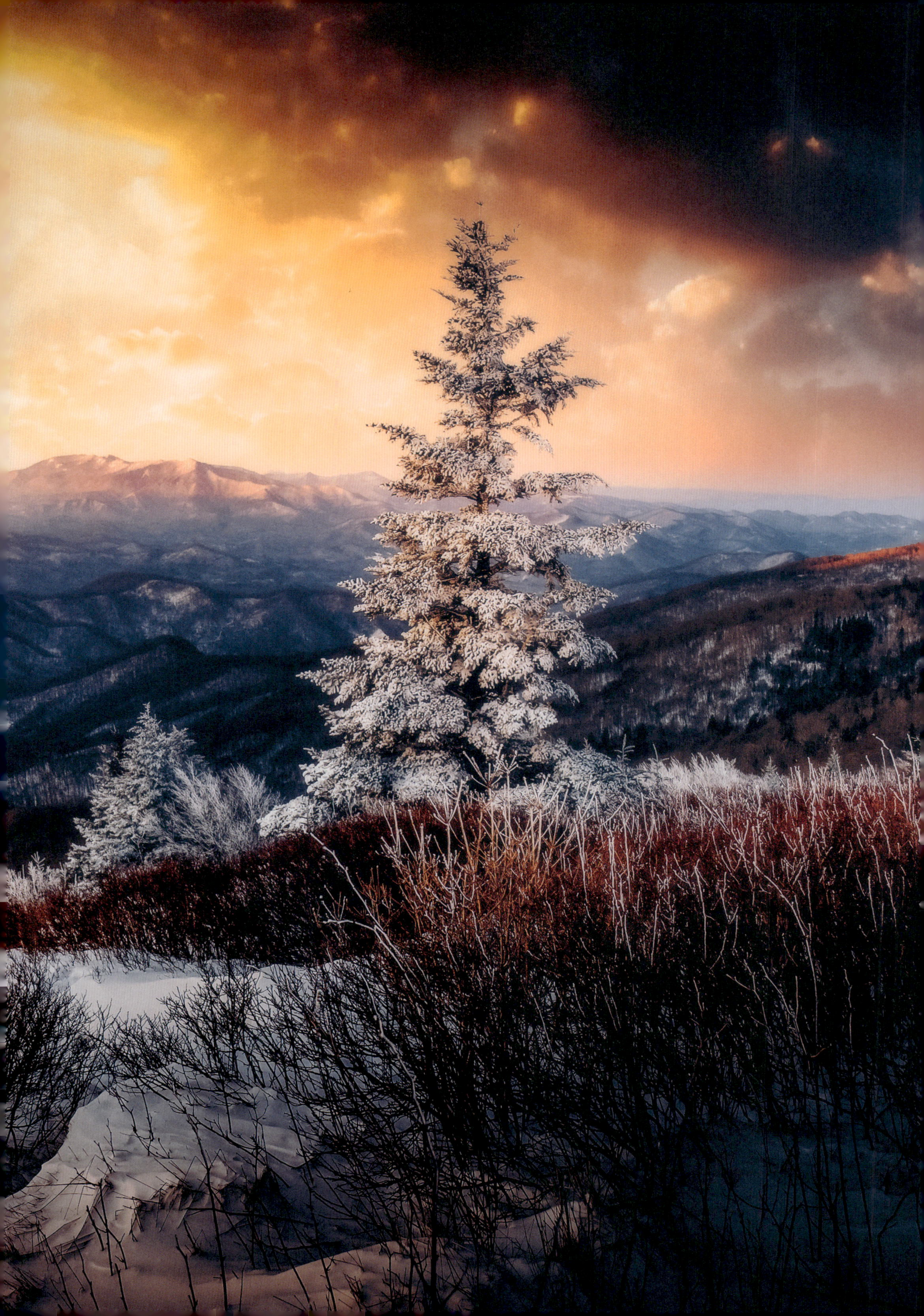

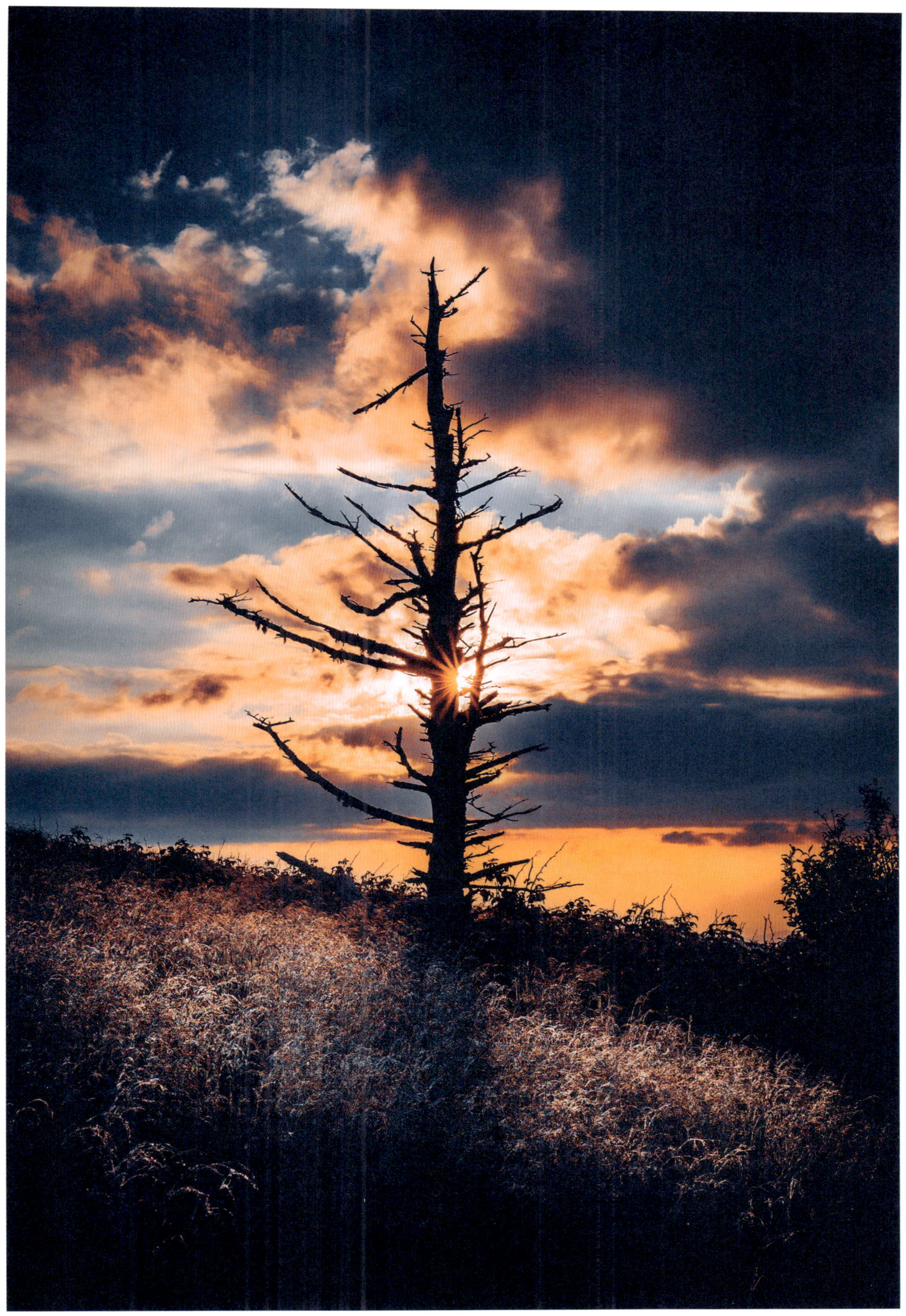

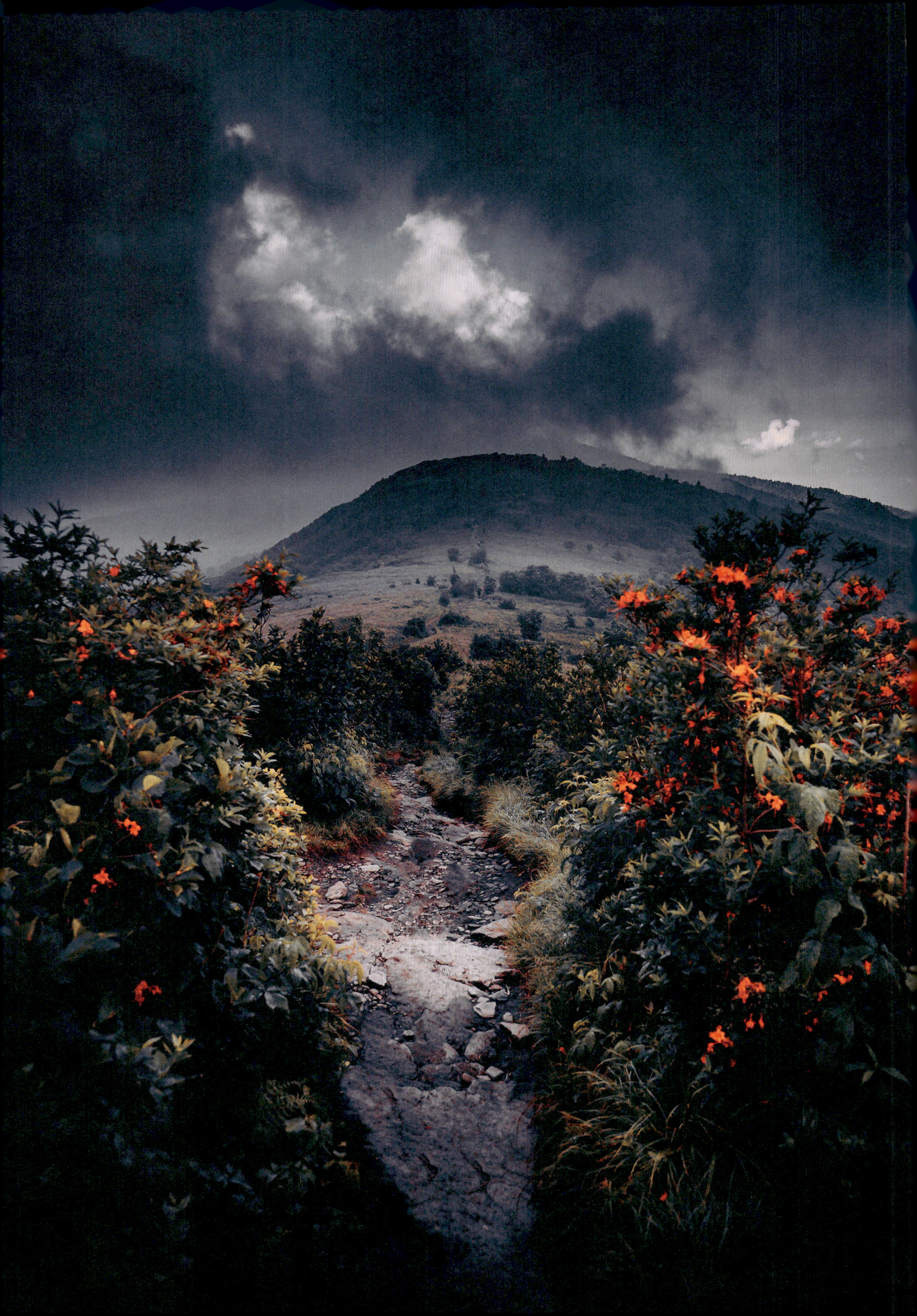

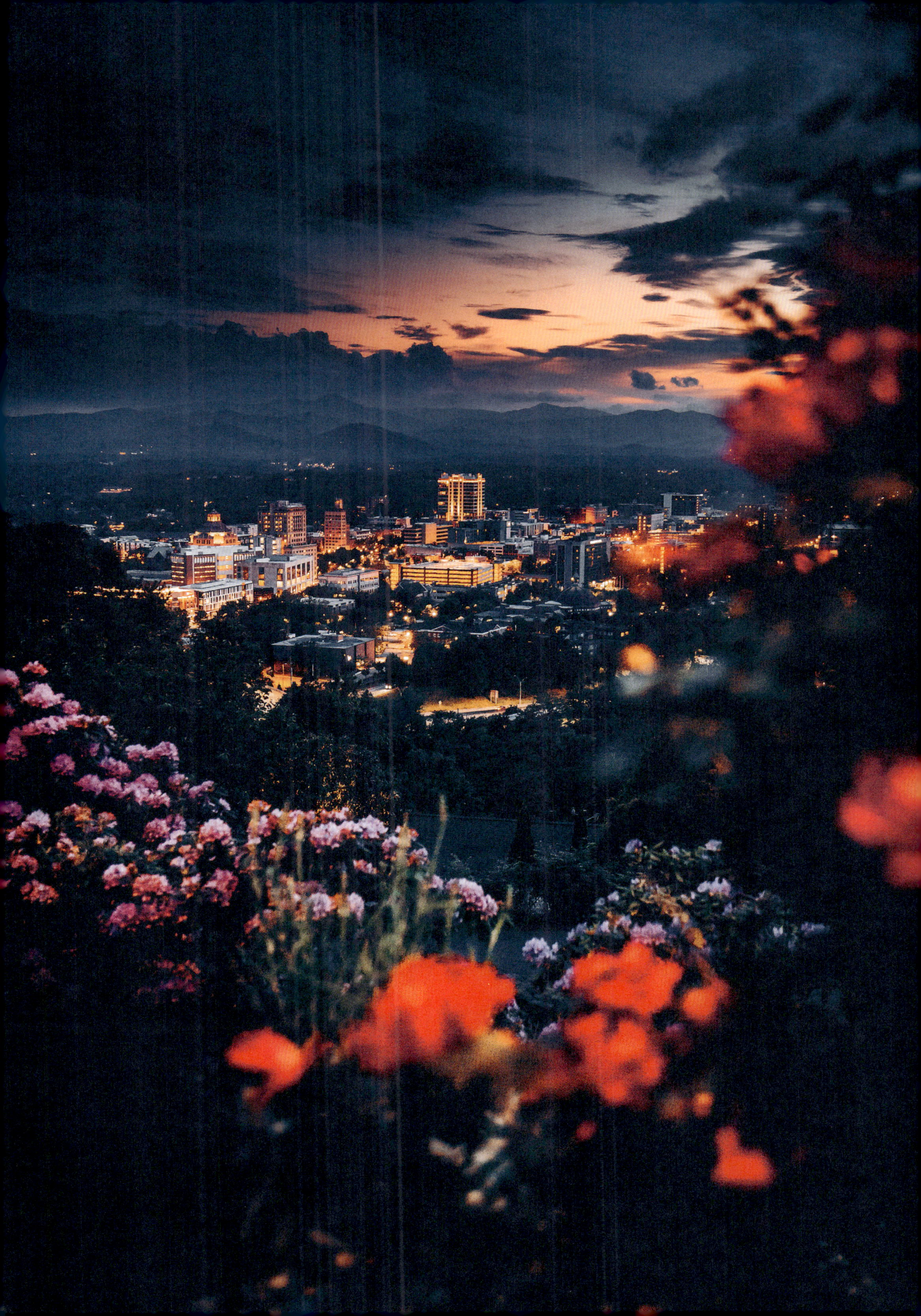

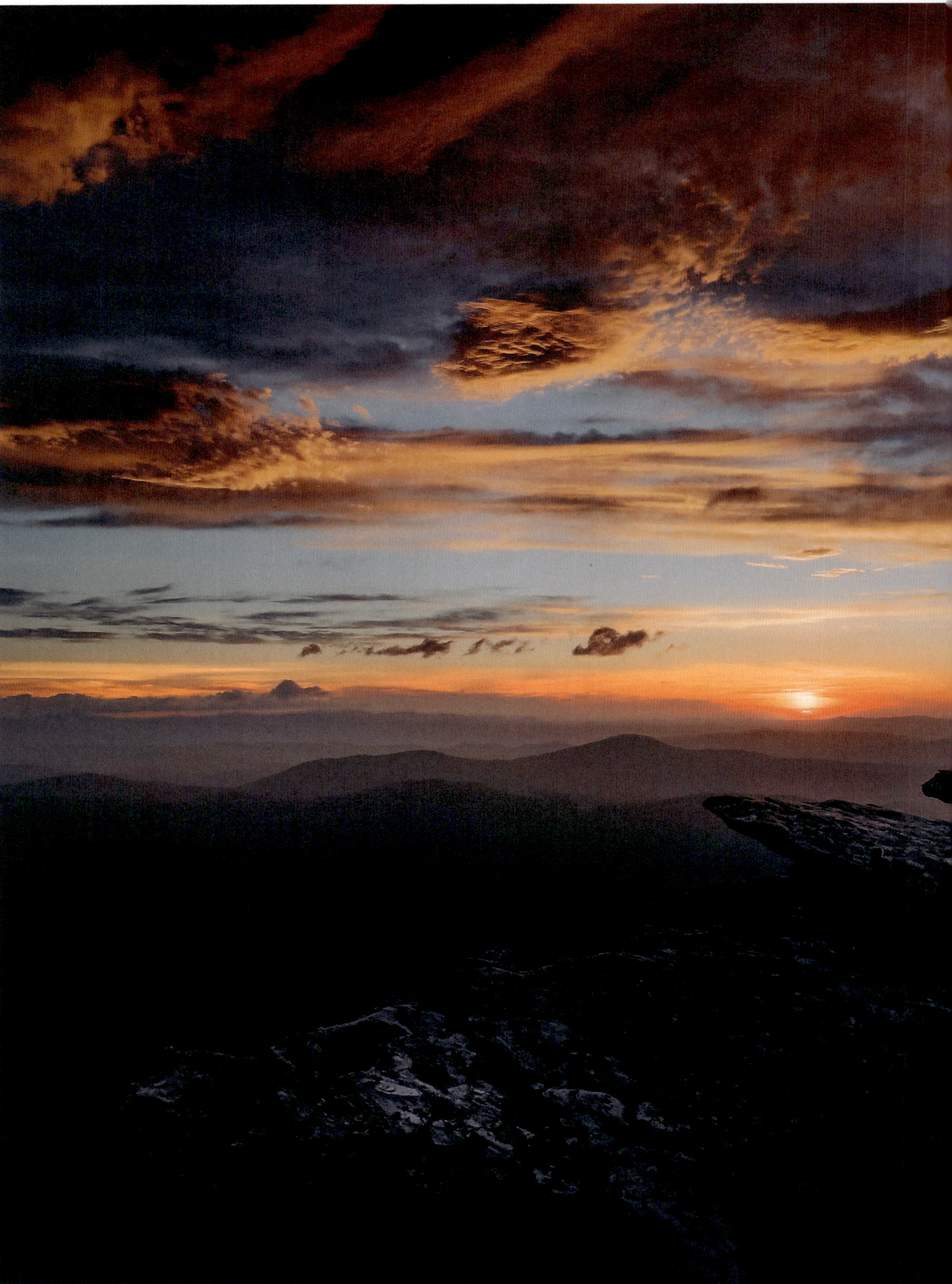

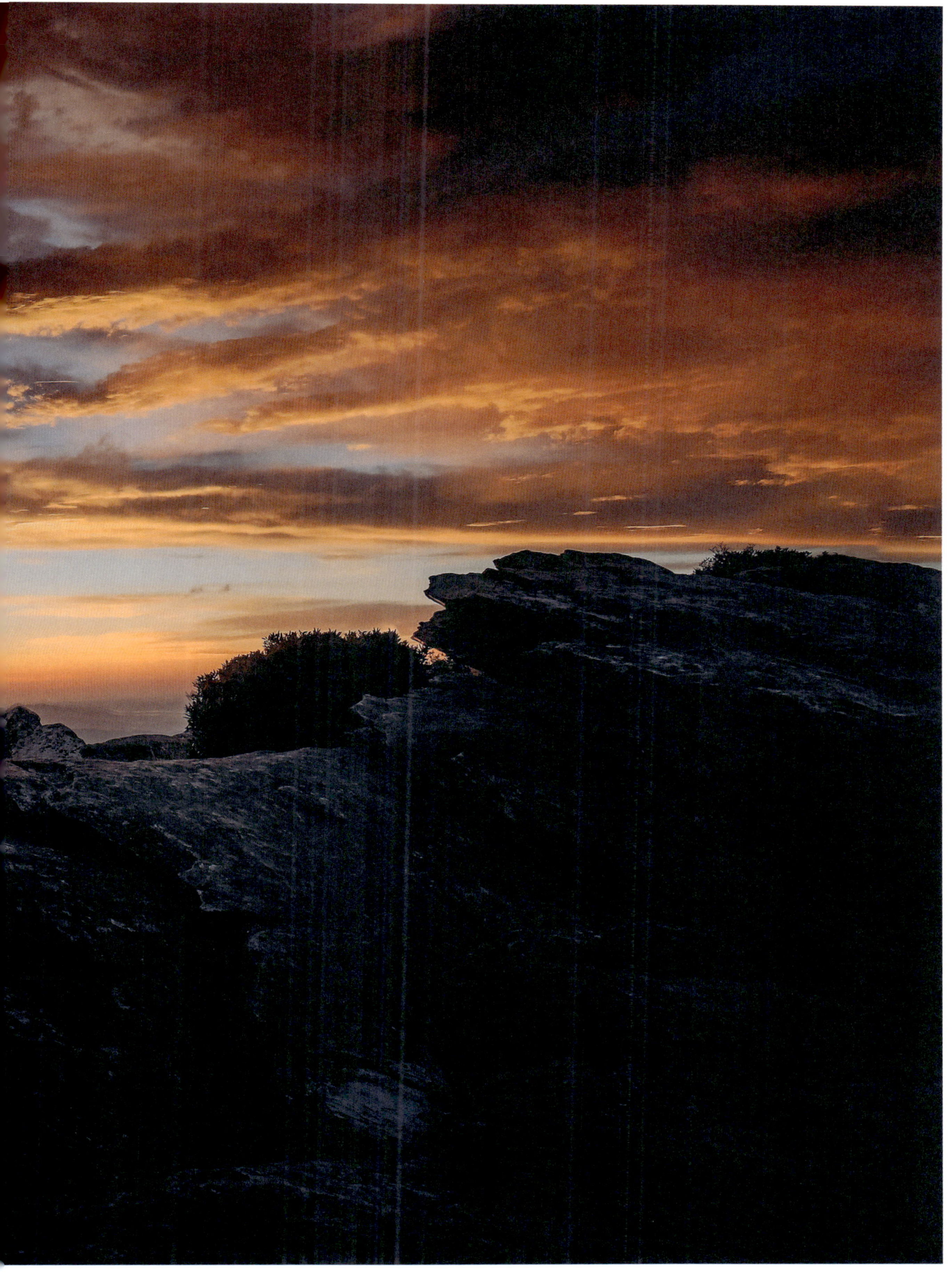

Alone Looking at the Mountain

All the birds have flown up and gone;
A lonely cloud floats leisurely by.
We never tire of looking at each other –
Only the mountain and I.

LI PO

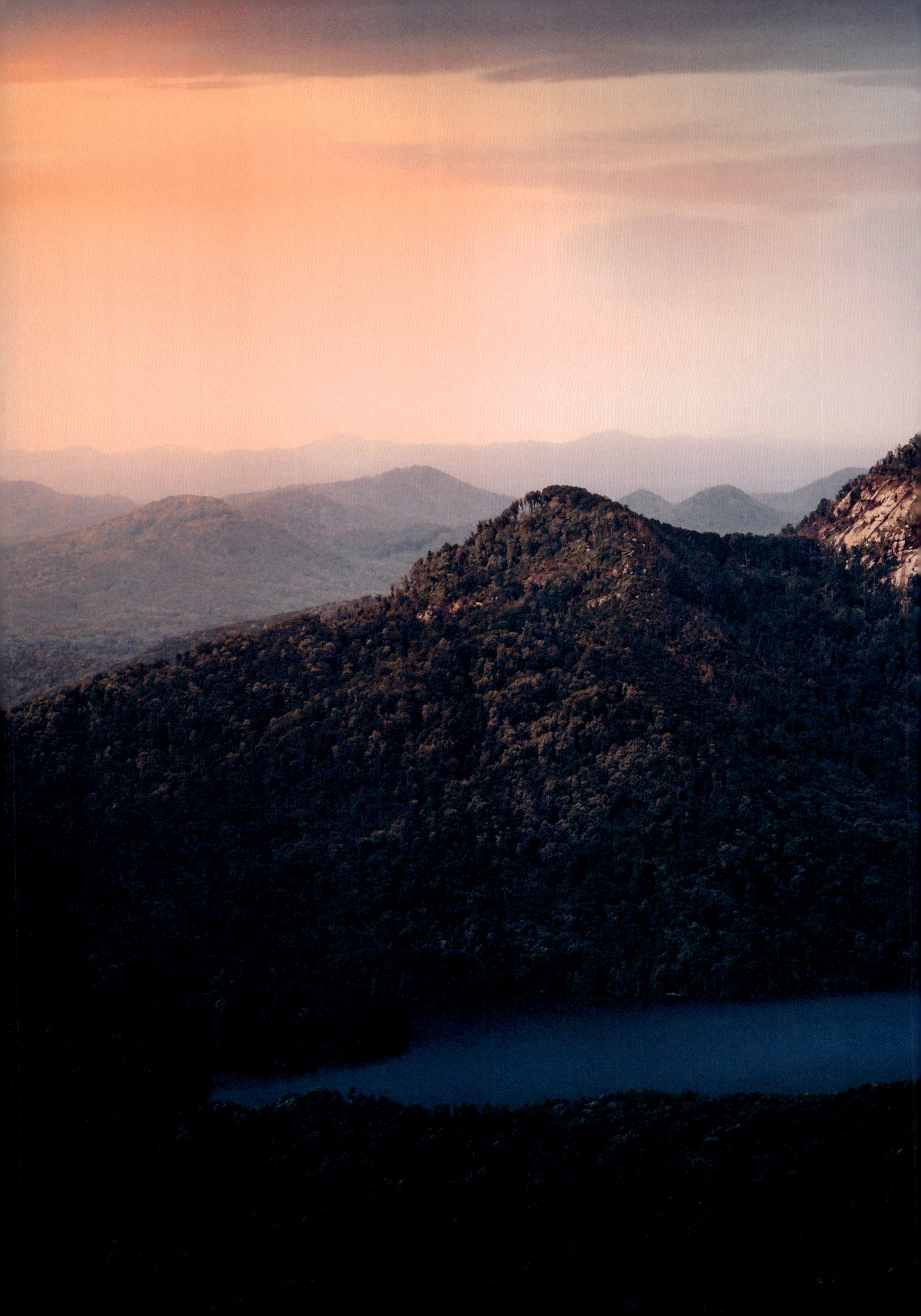

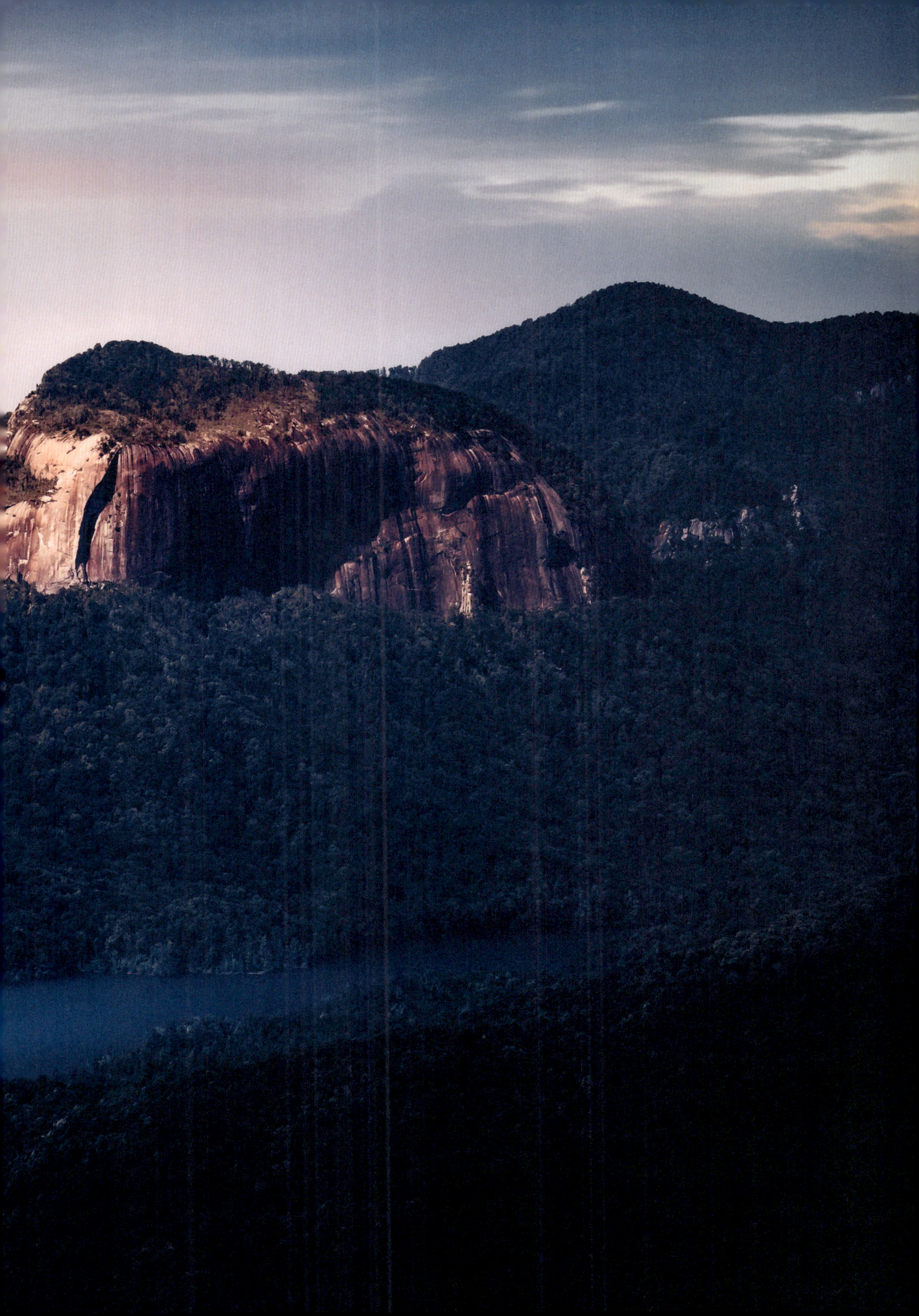

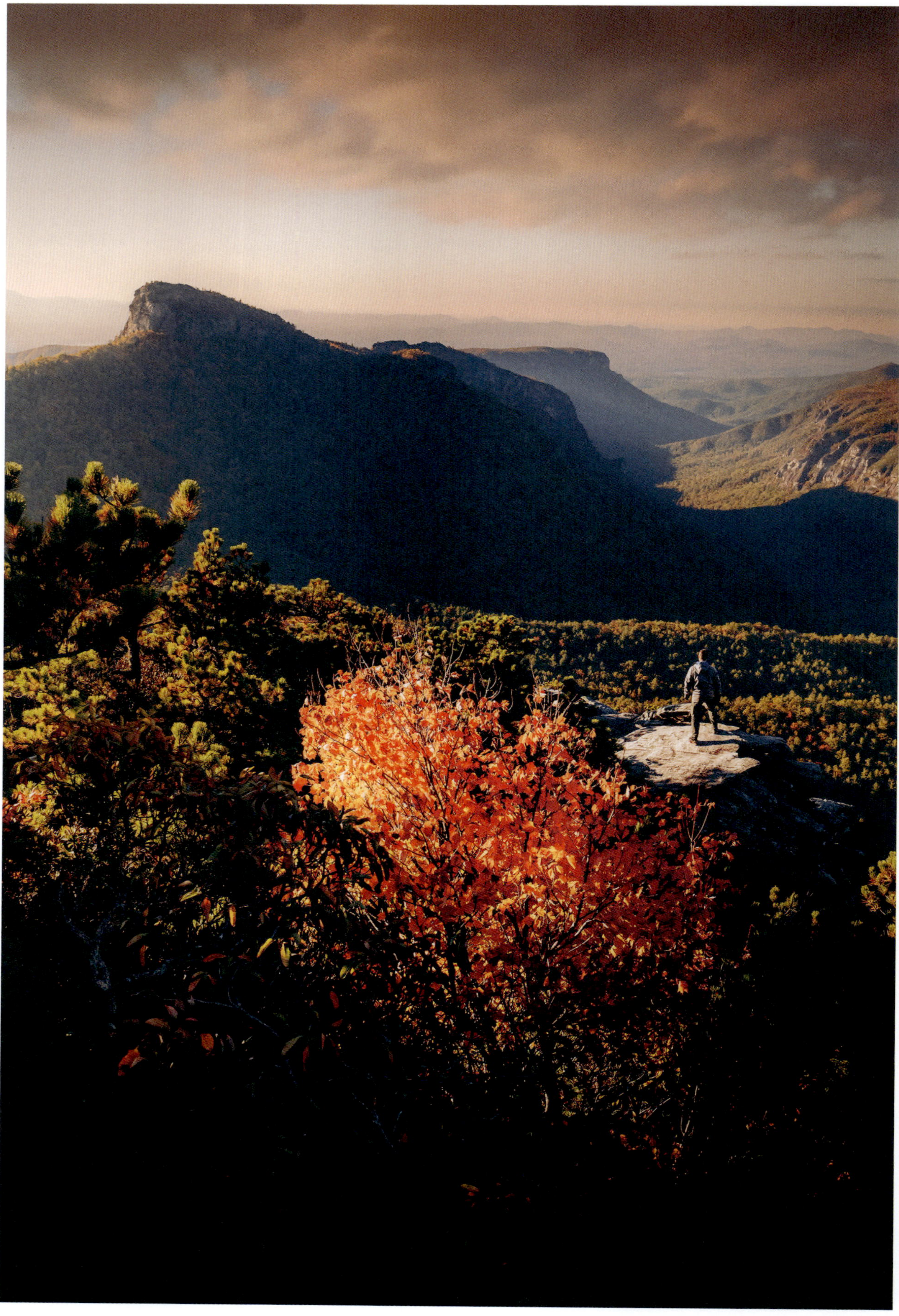

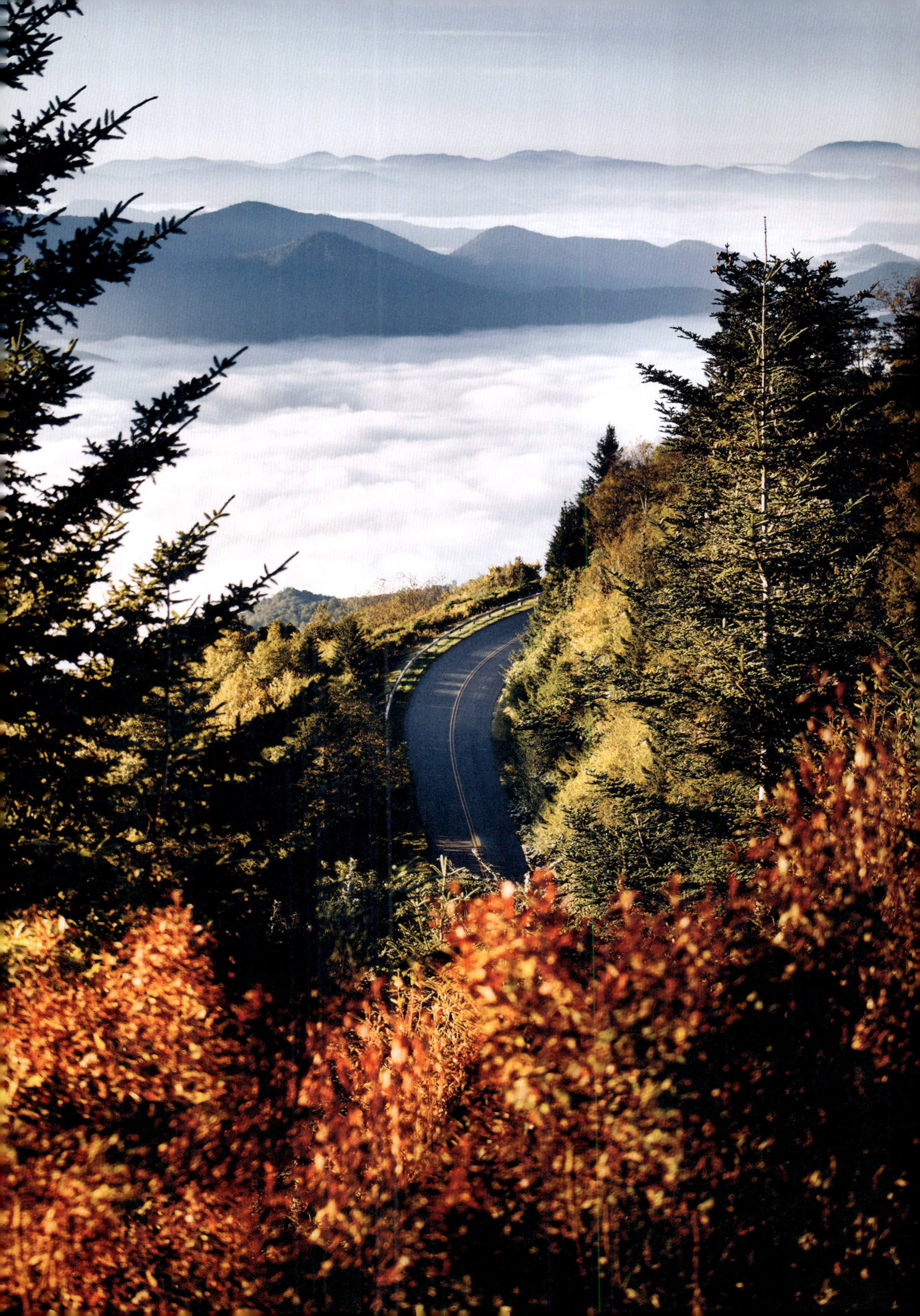

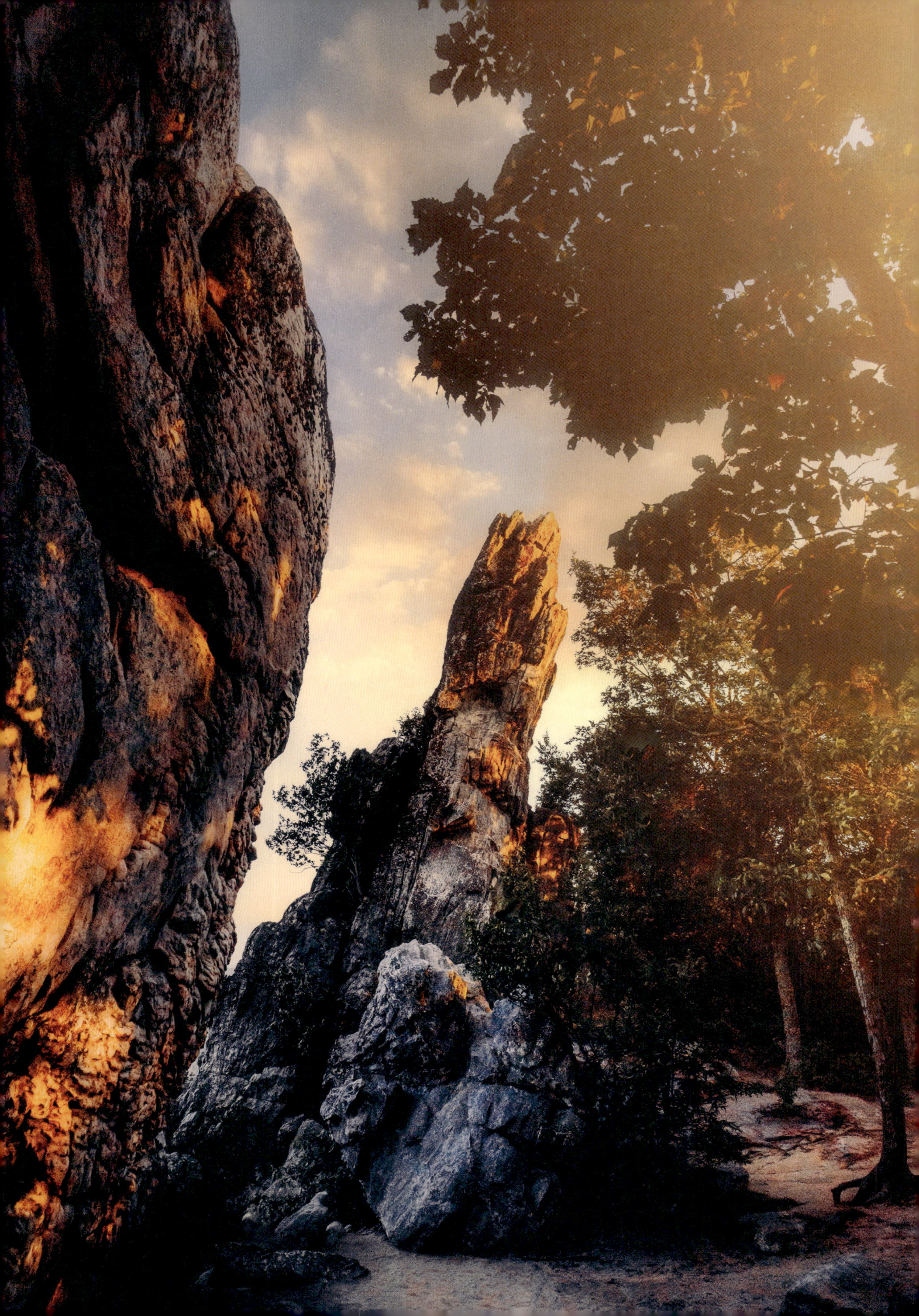

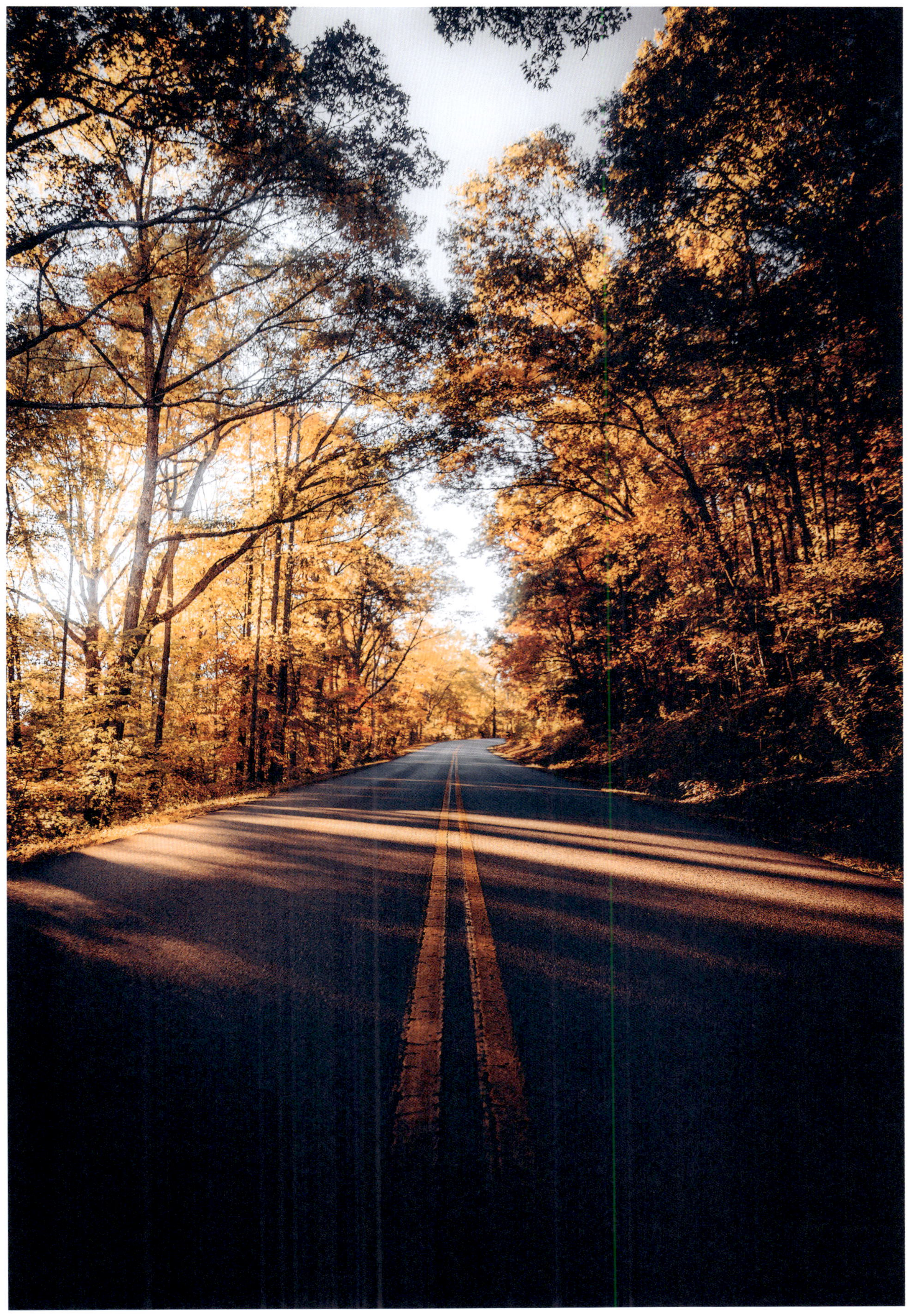

No spring nor
summer beauty
hath such grace

As I have seen in
one autumnal face.

JOHN DONNE

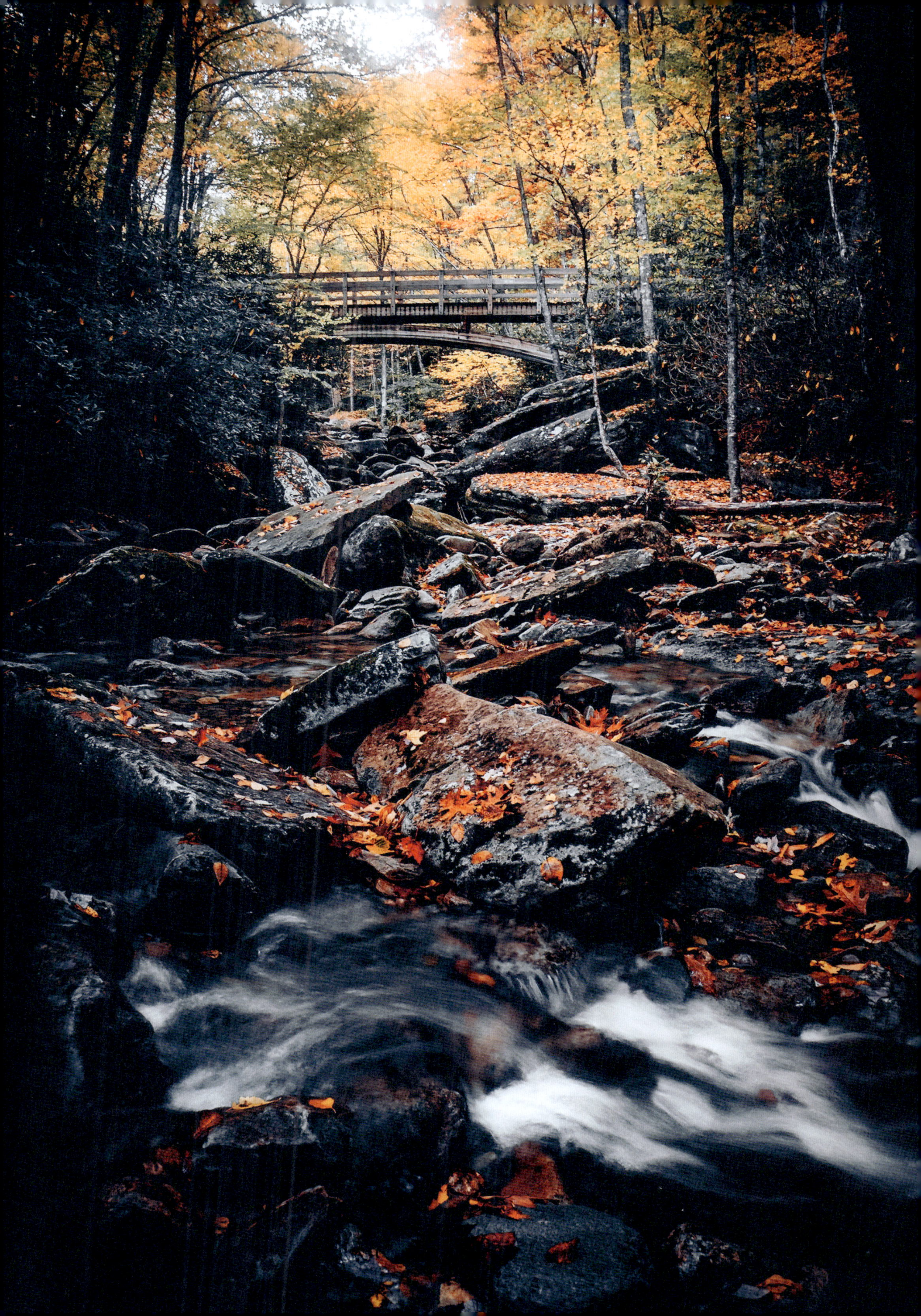

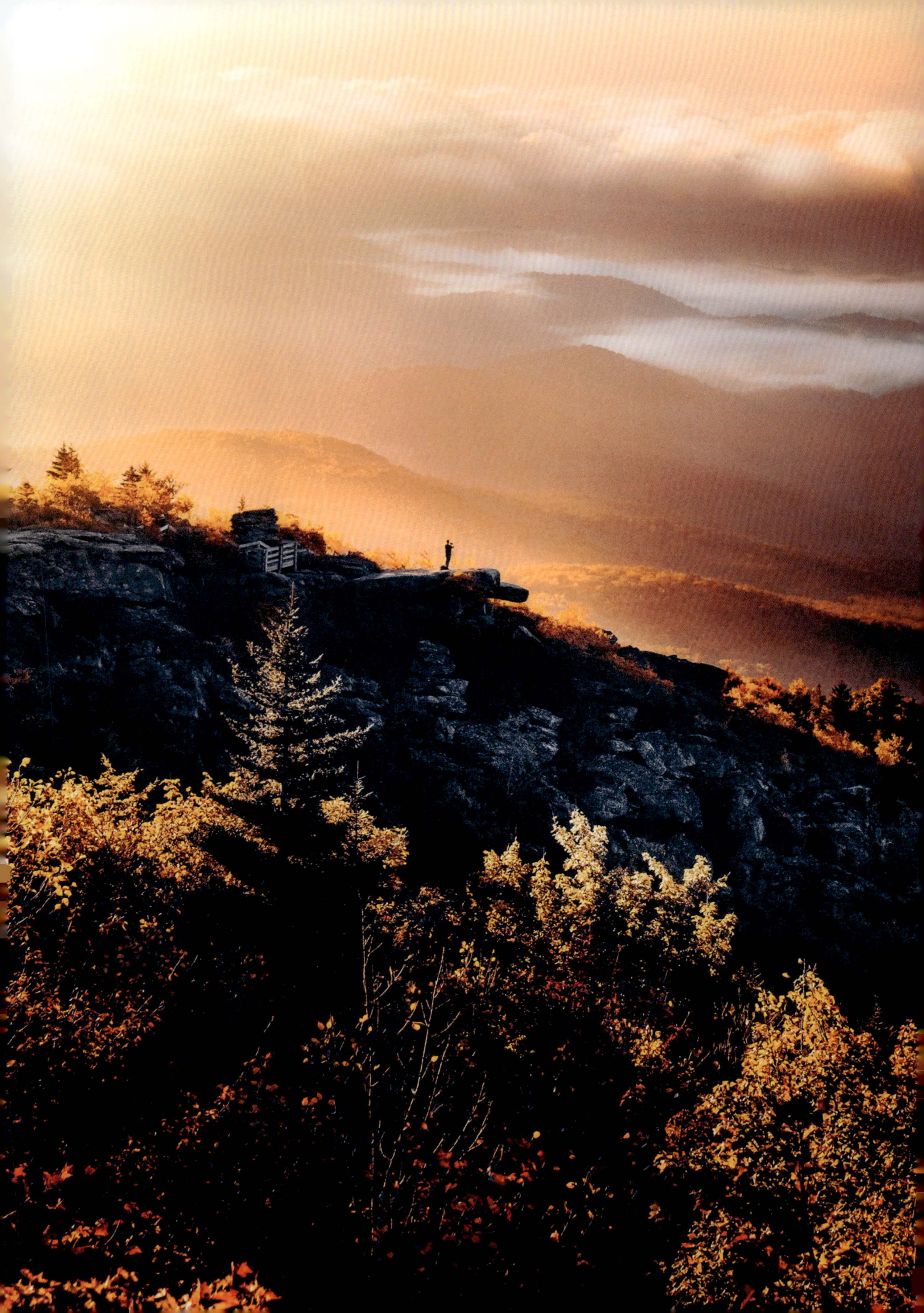

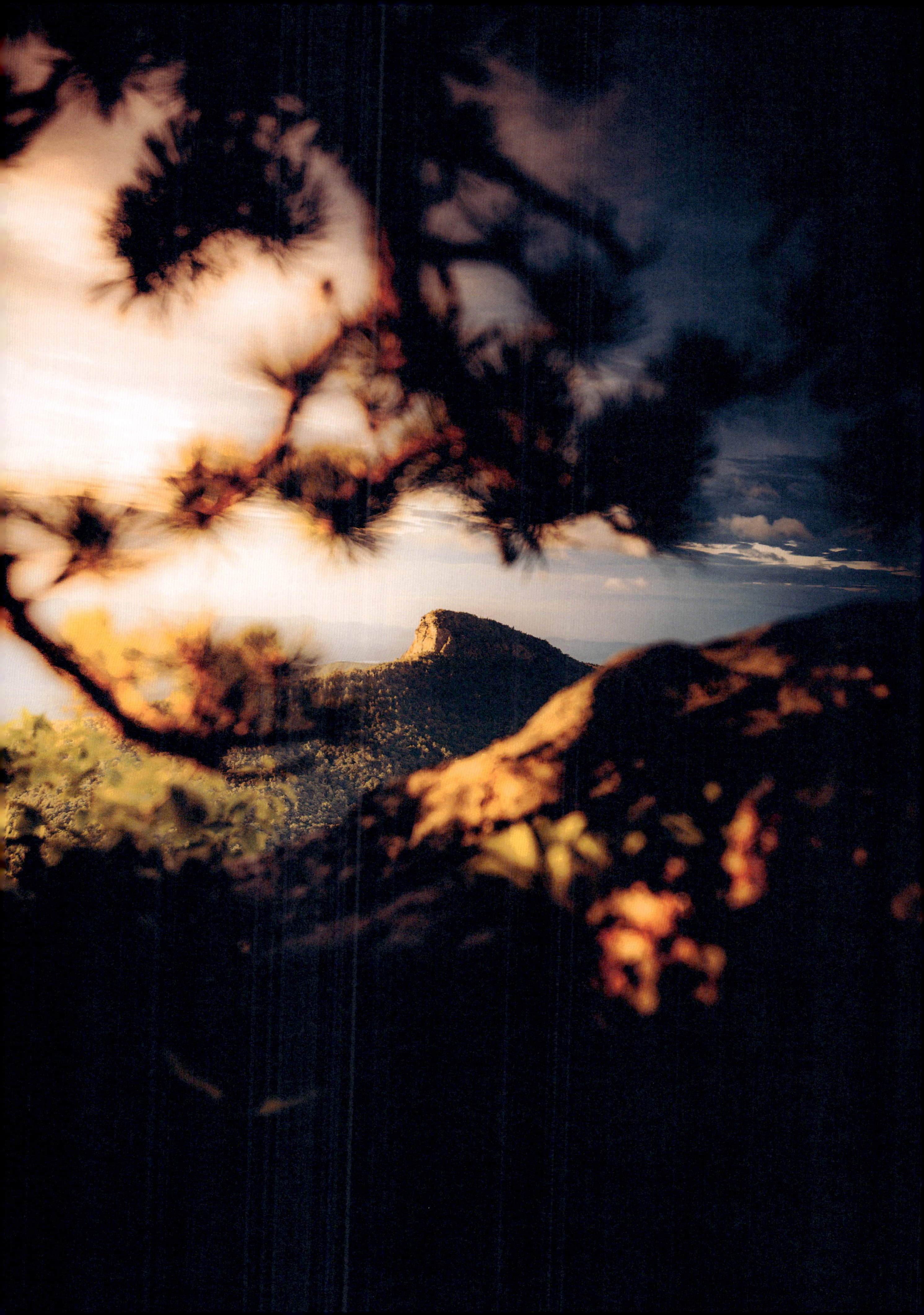

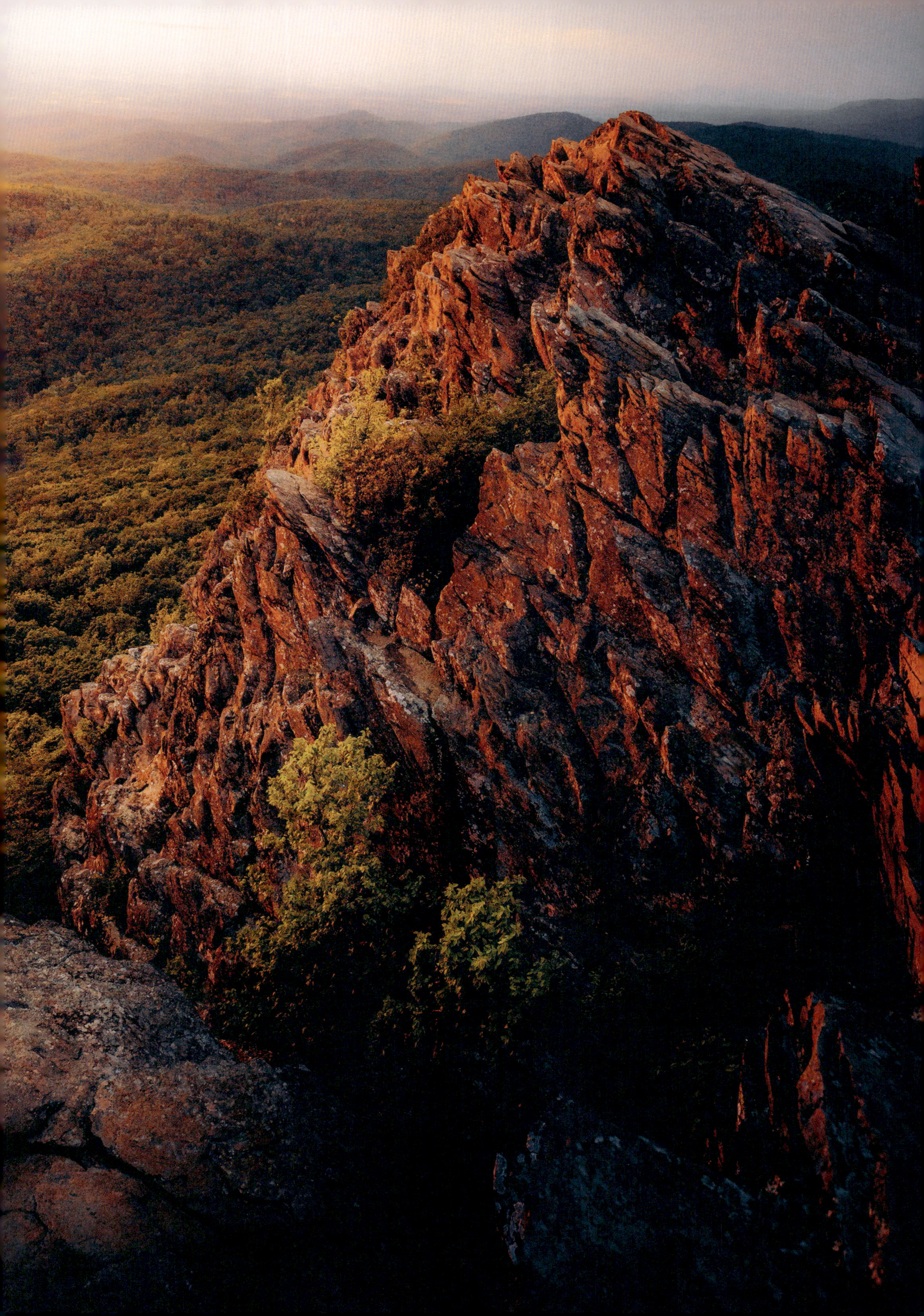

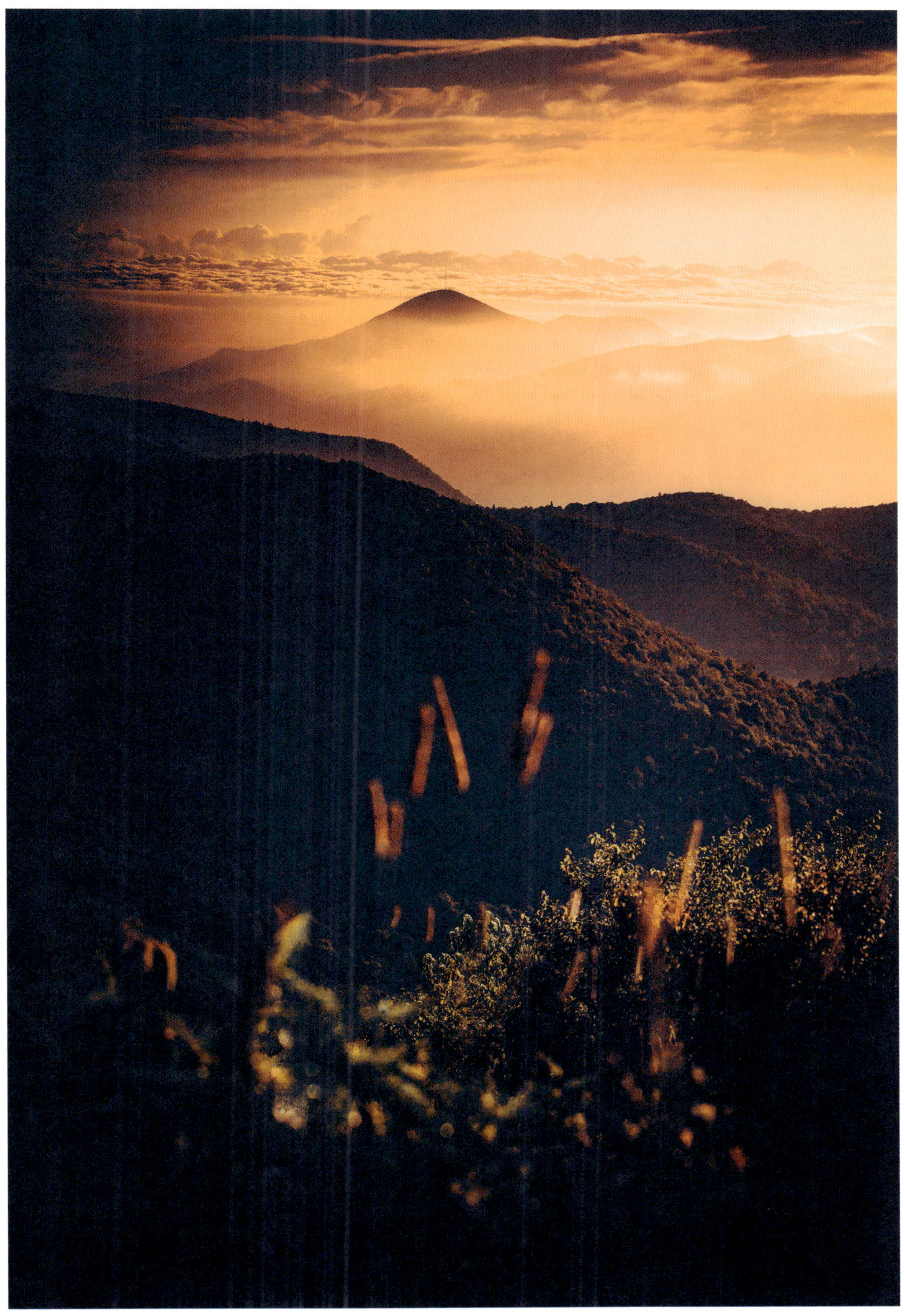

Going to the mountains
is like going home.

JOHN MUIR

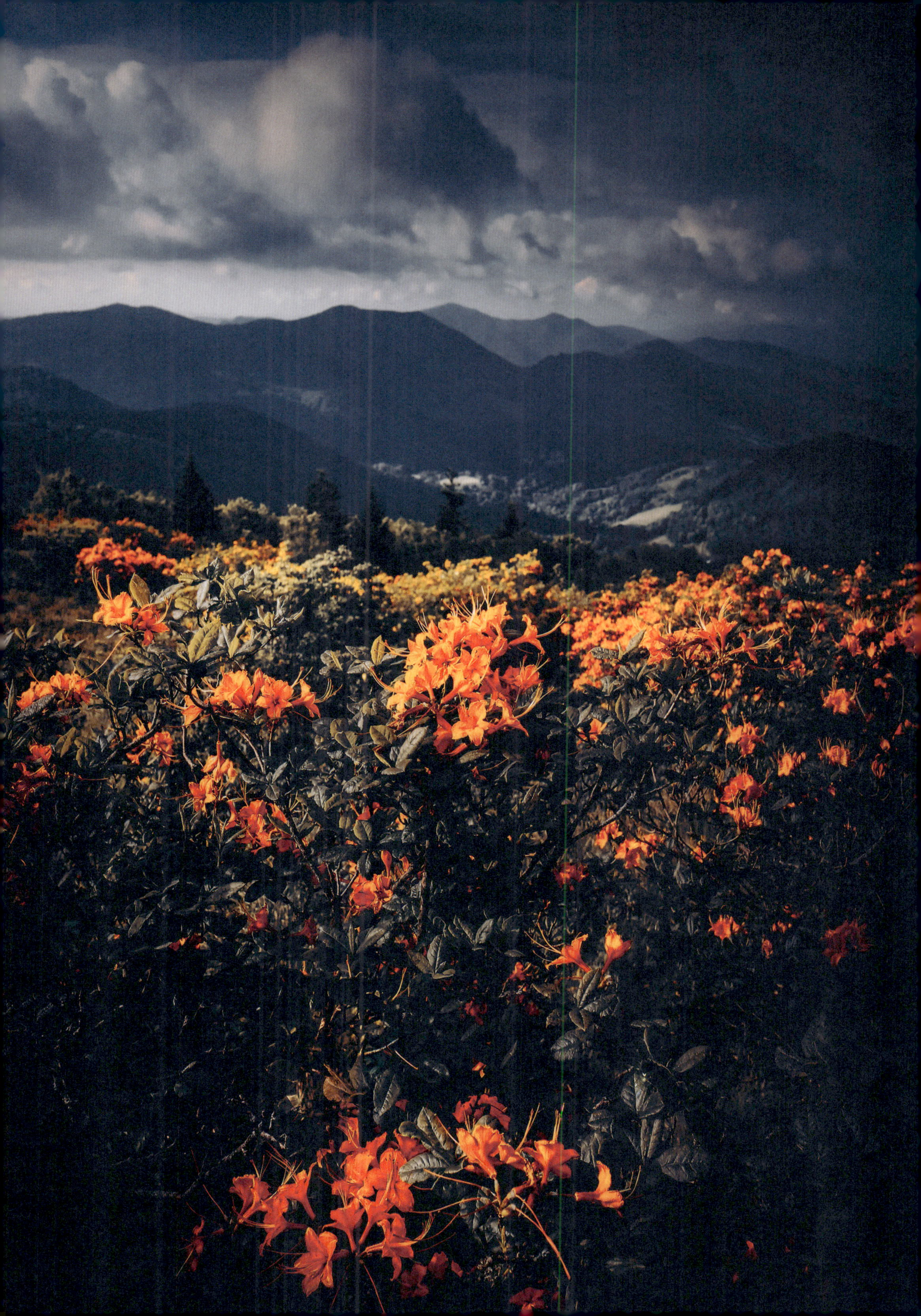

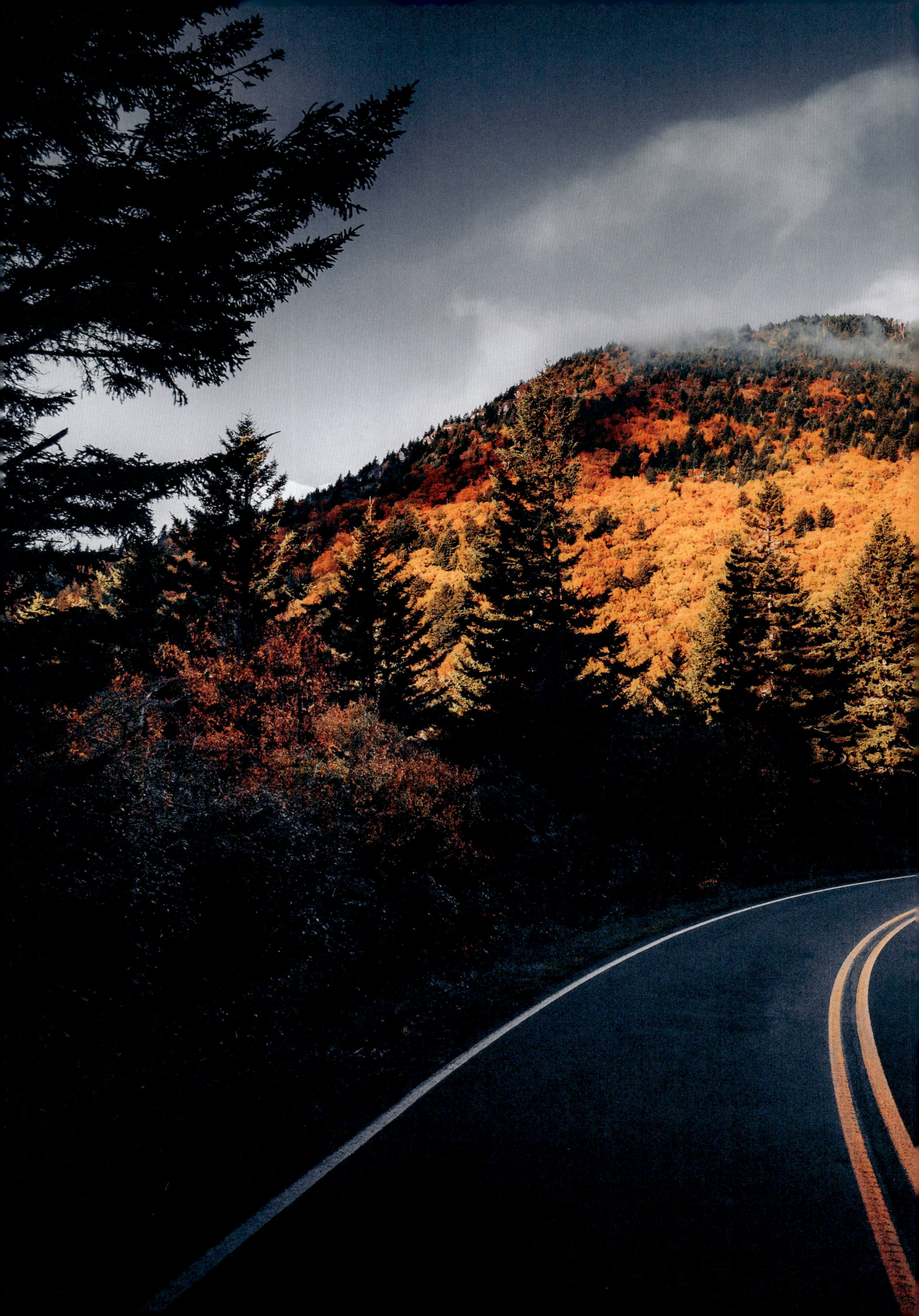

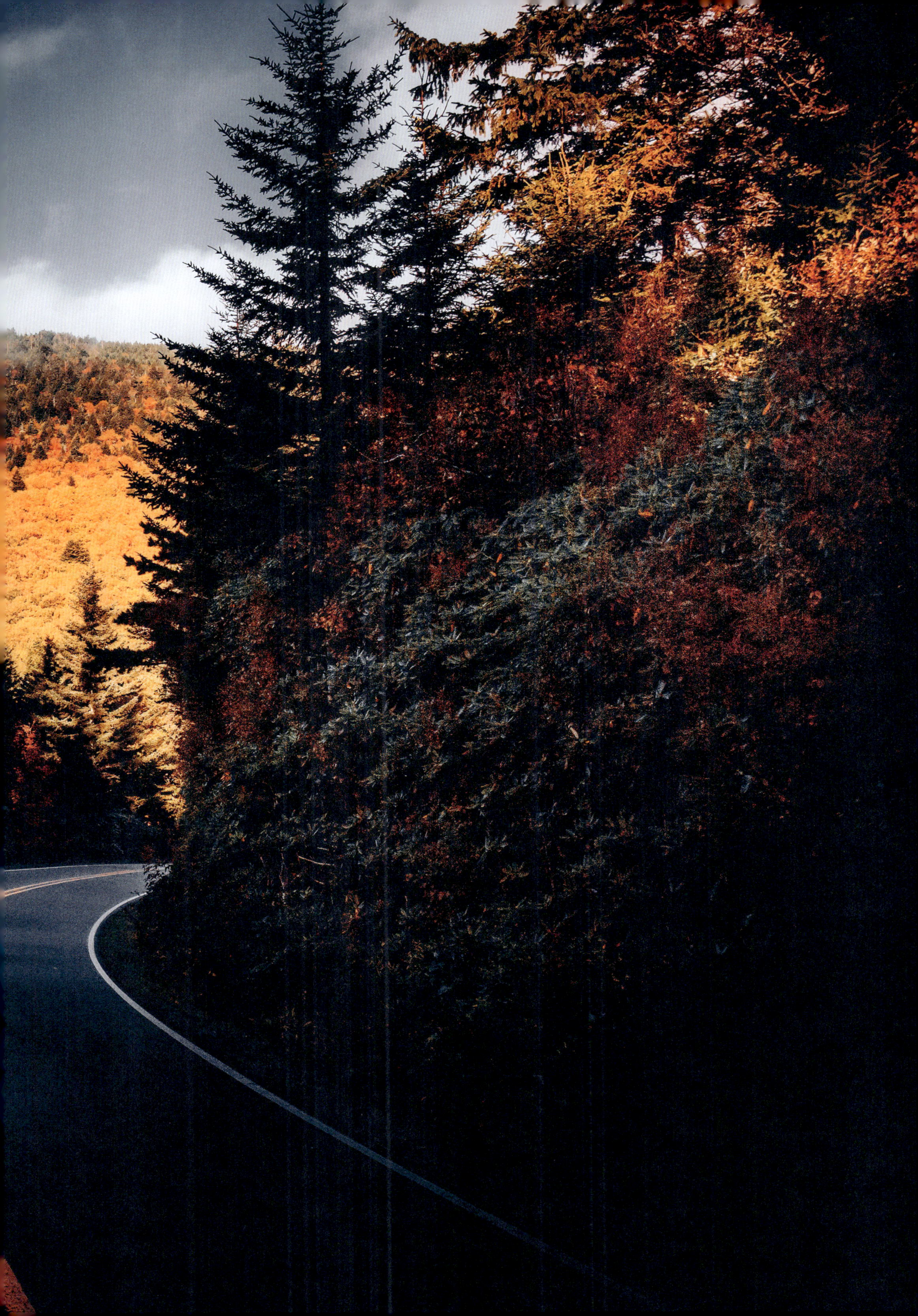

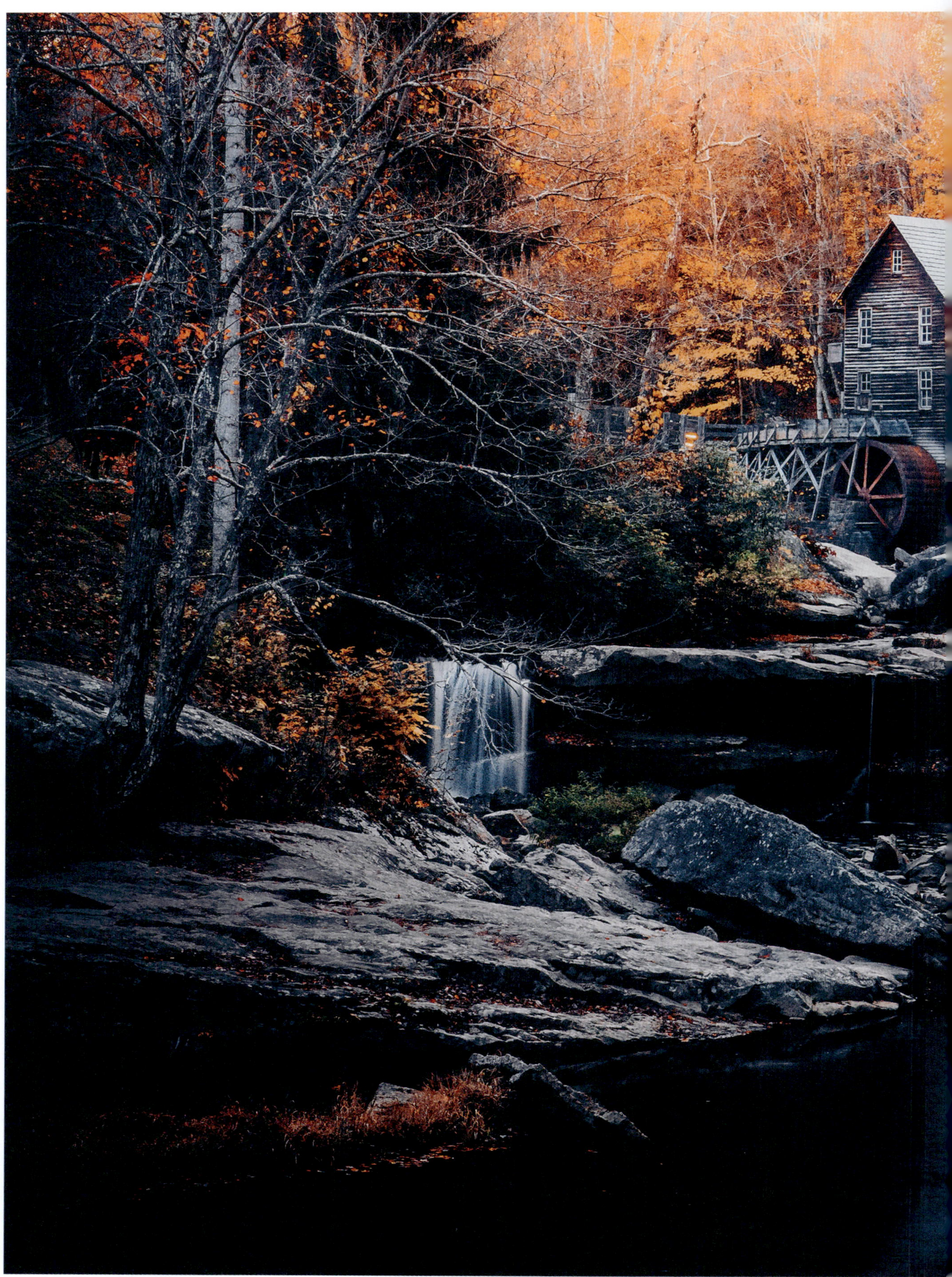

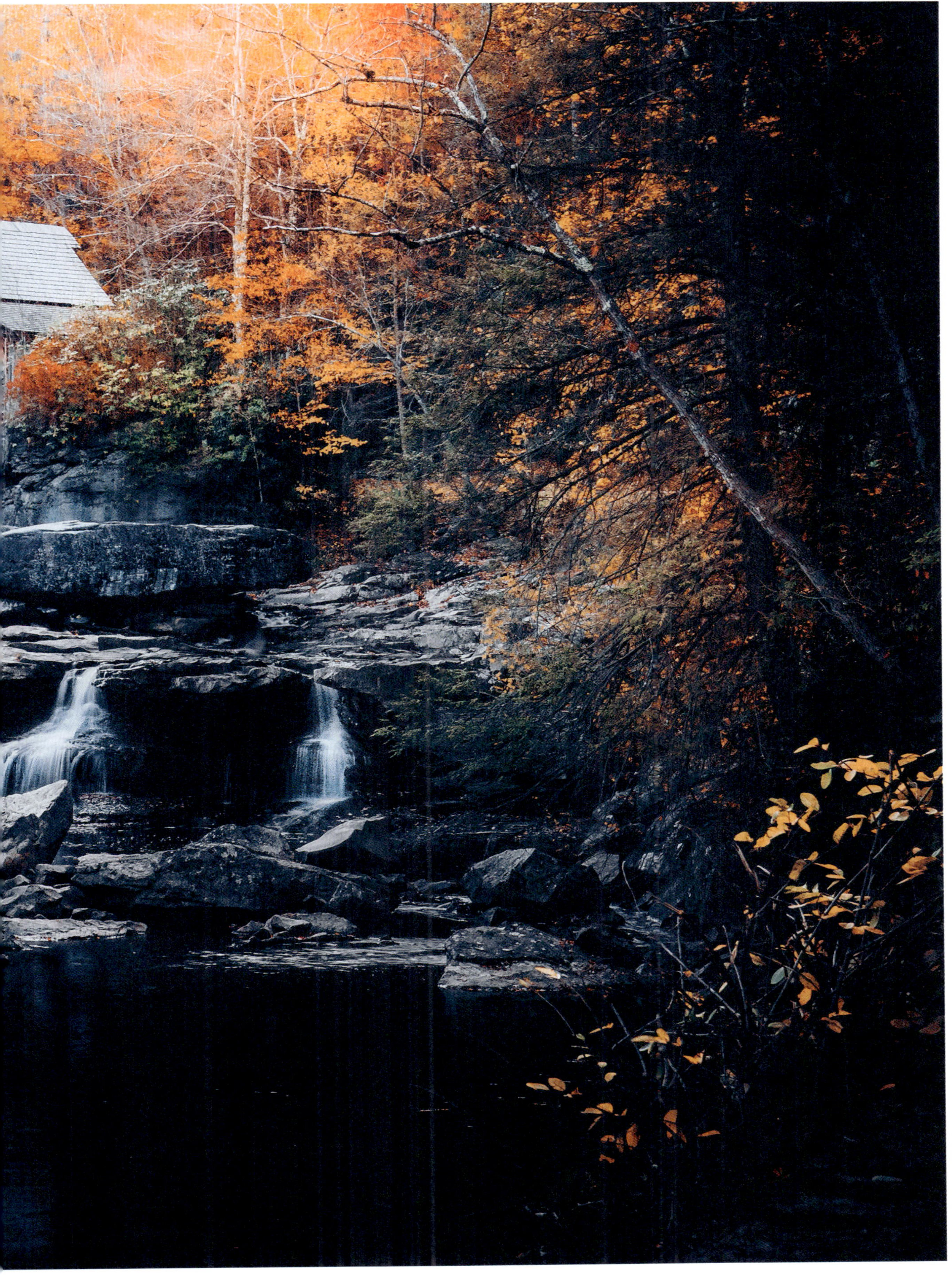

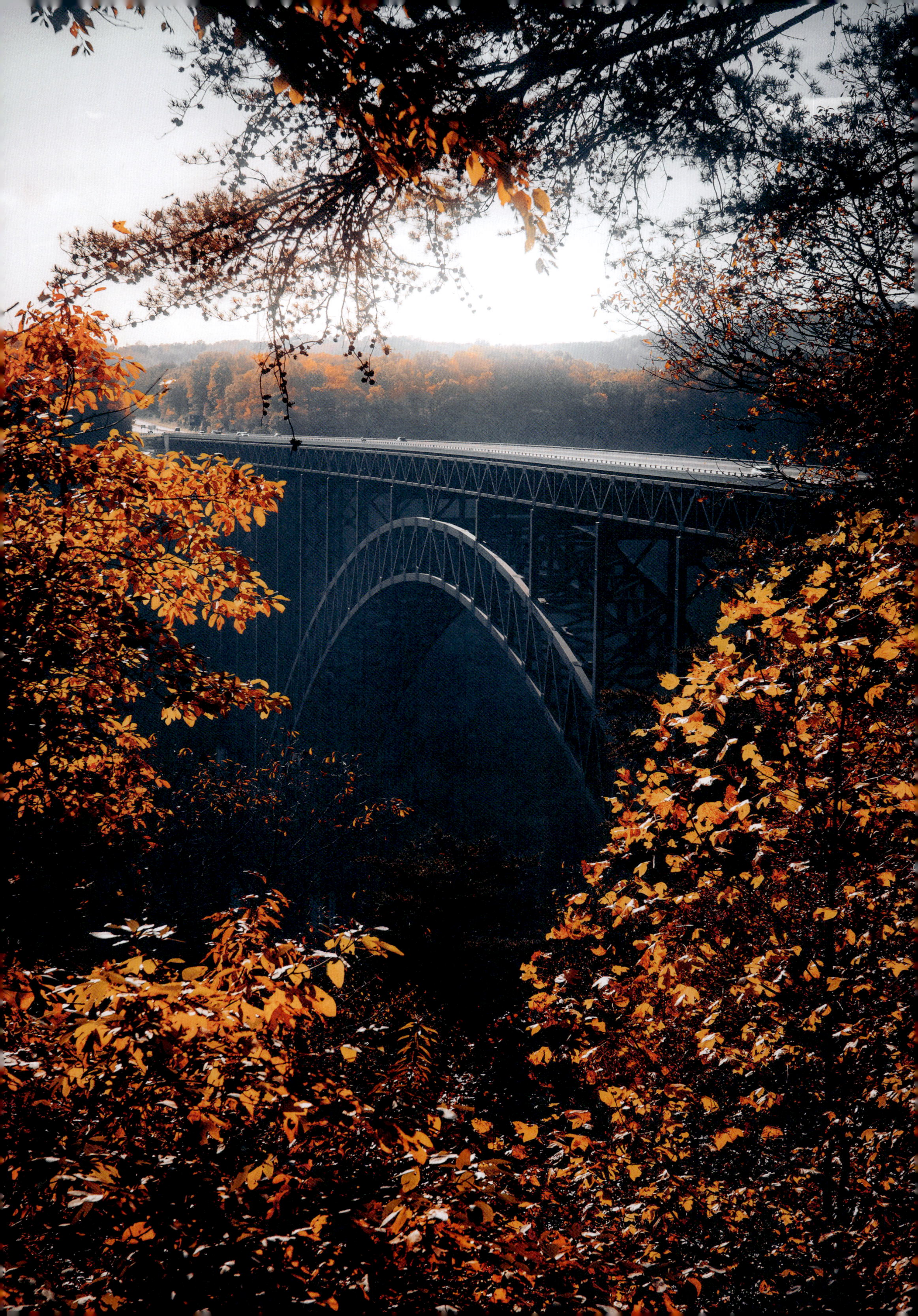

Breathtaking Delight

blue ridge mountains soar
lifts me up from my lowest
breathtaking delight

MARTY KING

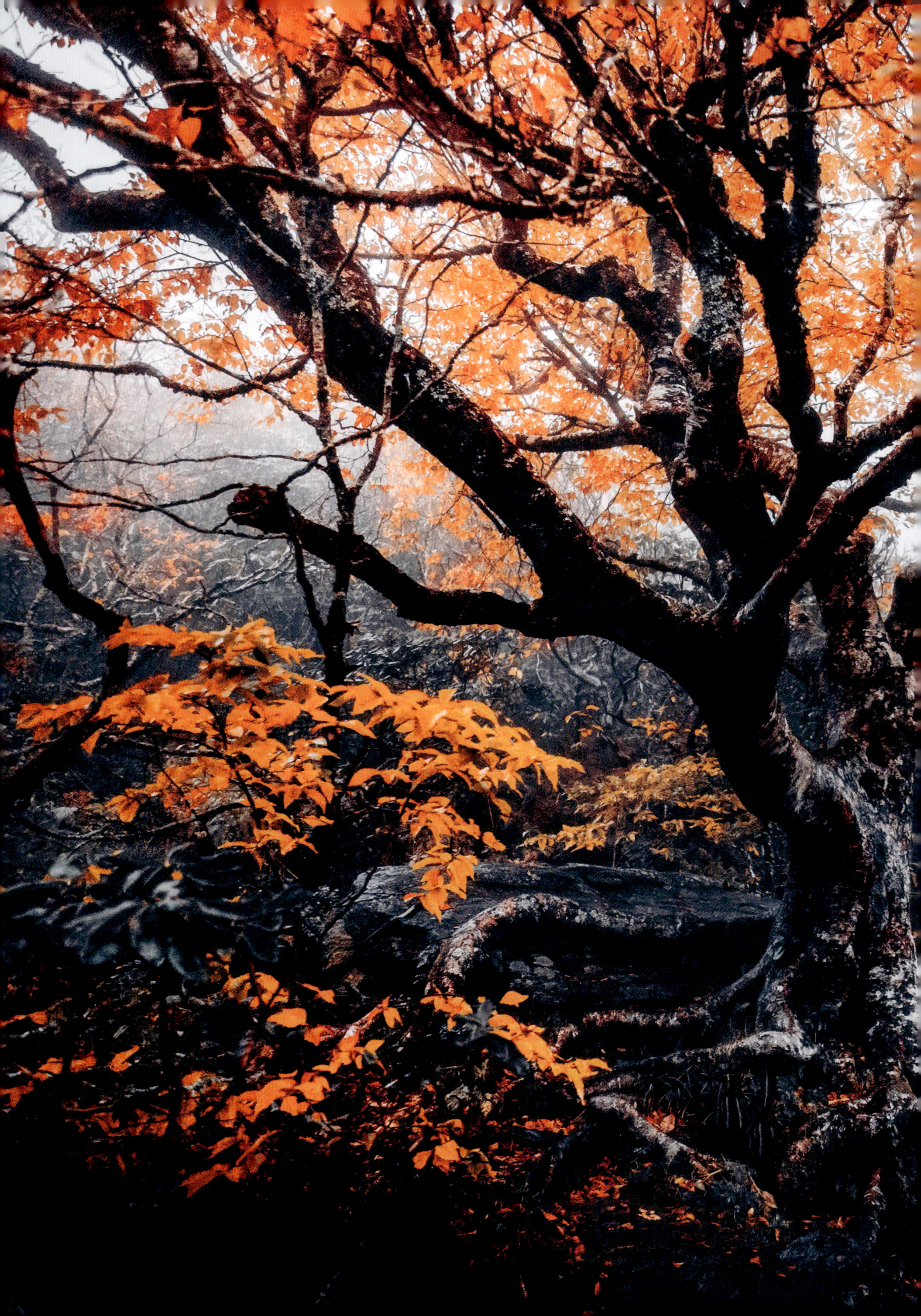

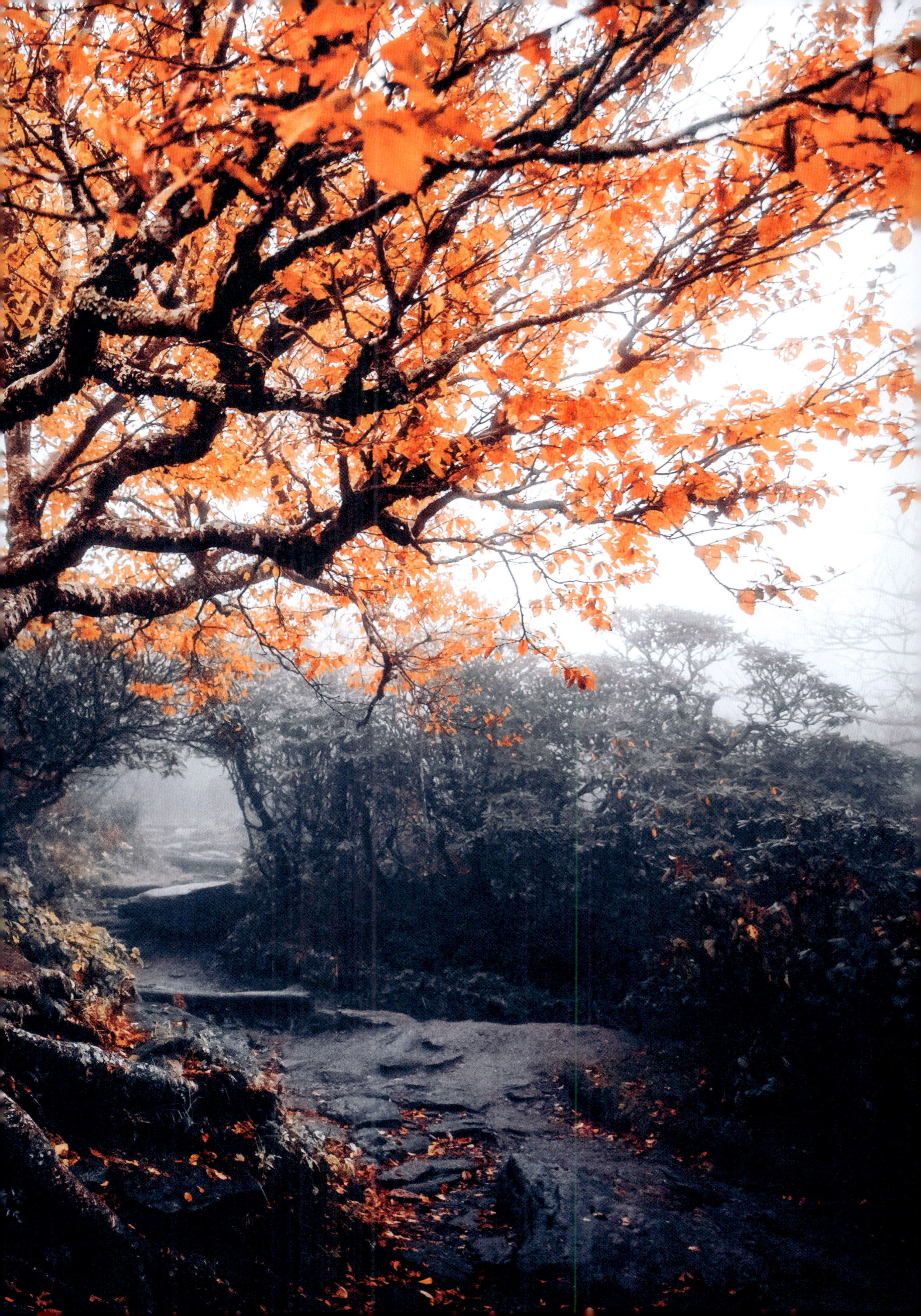

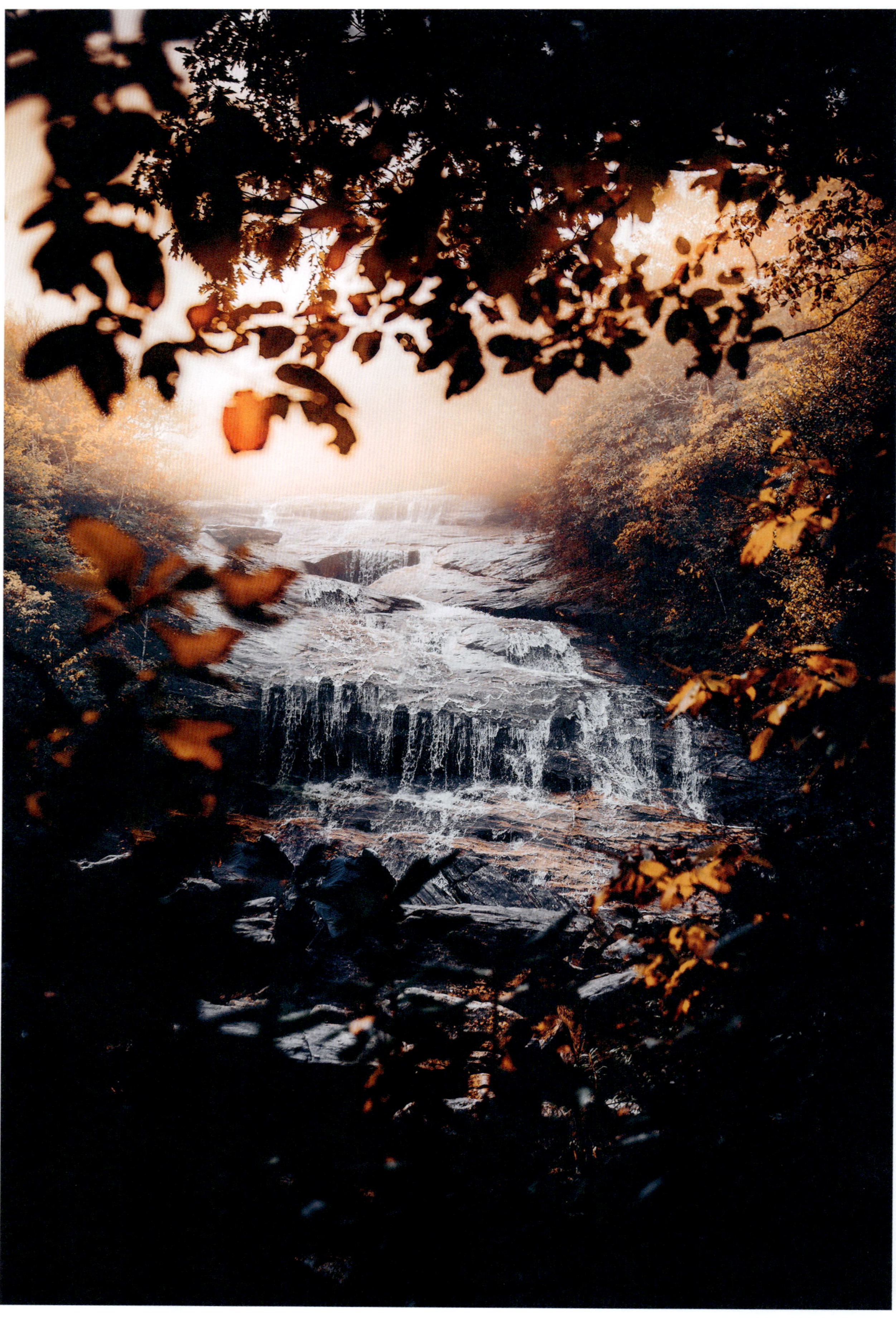

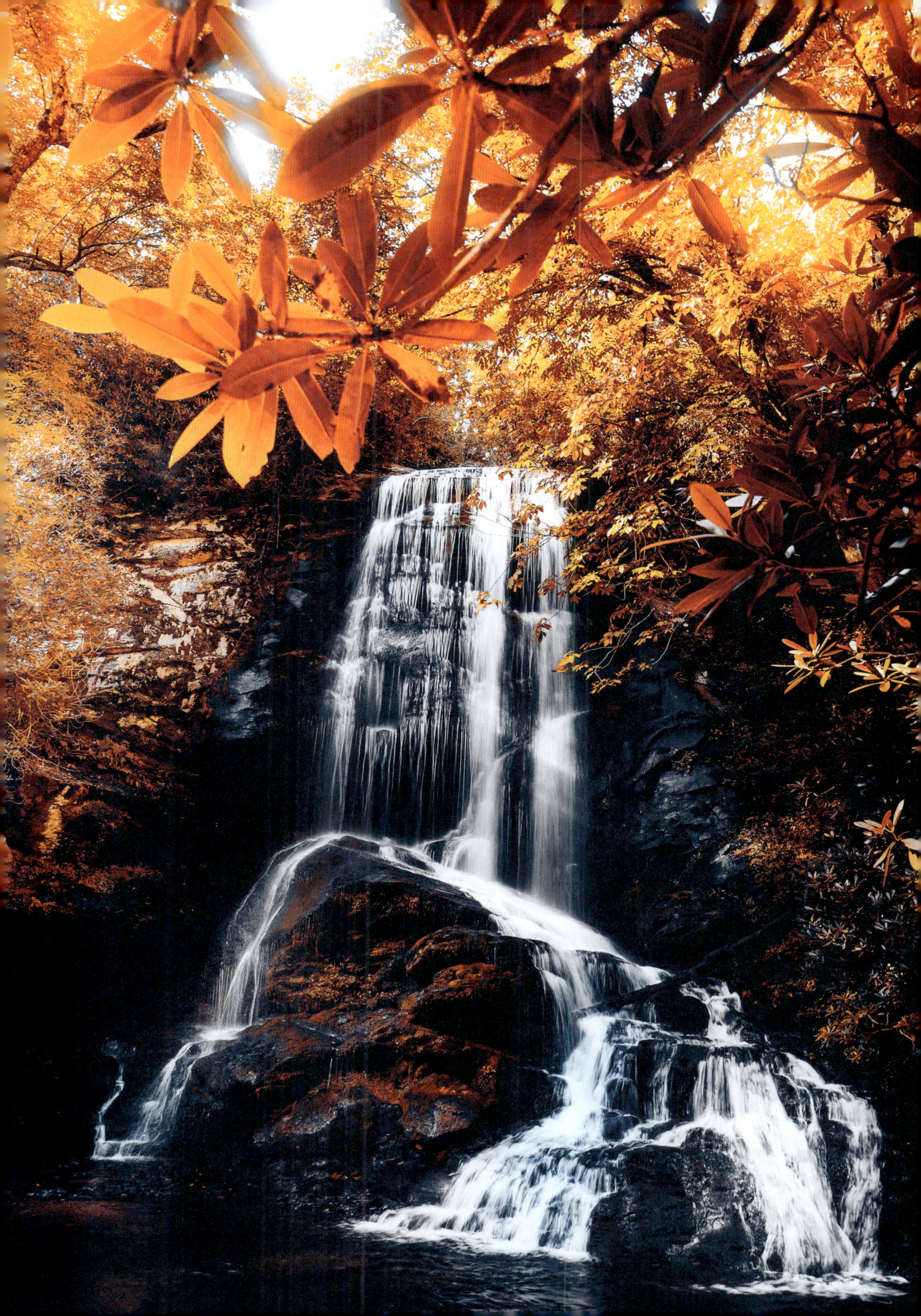

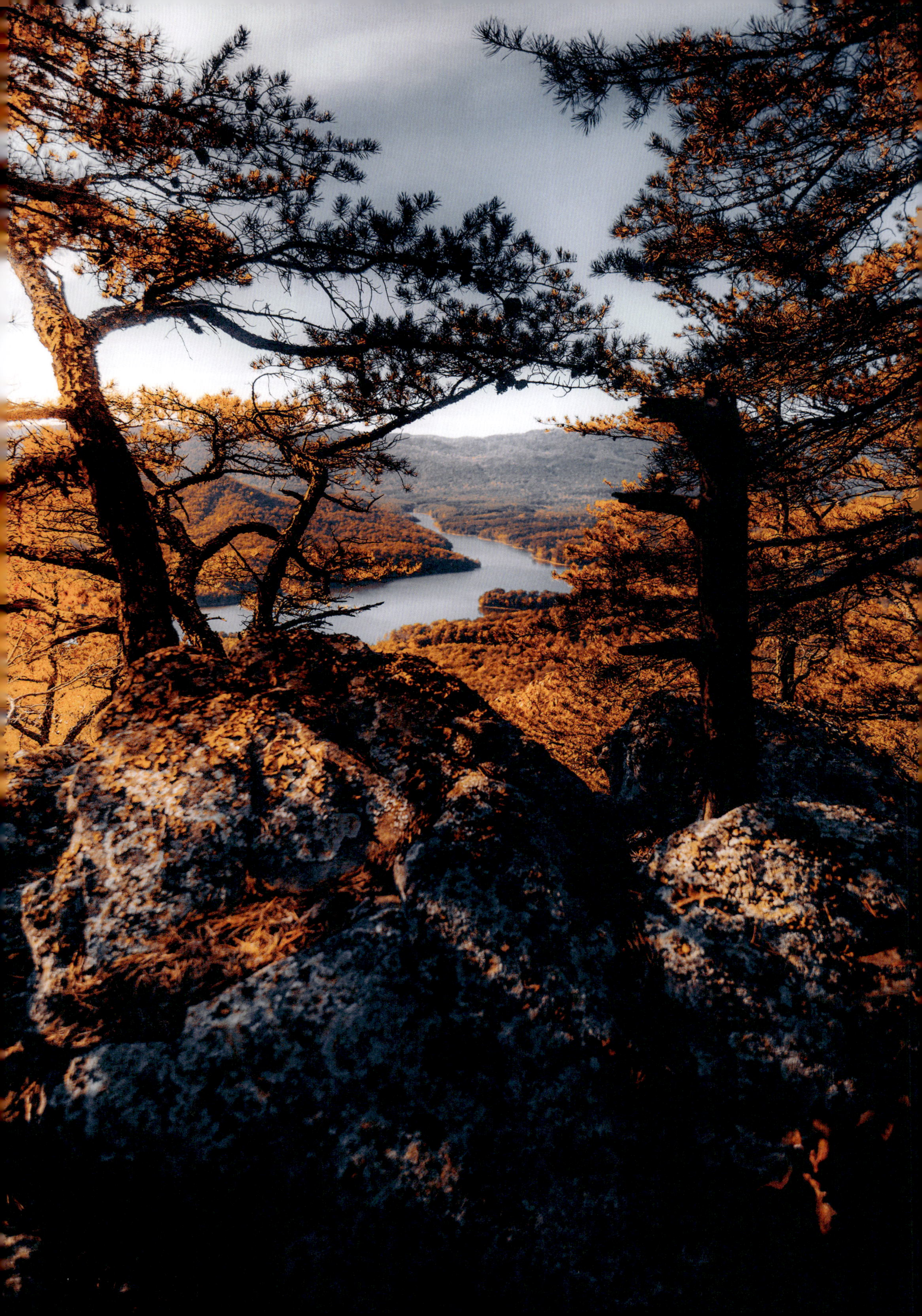

Blue Ridge Mountains (Excerpt)

Across the edges of the blue ridges
Caressing the emerald pine and whispering
Gentle thoughts through the birch
Calming hearts with this mysterious touch
From the fiery paintbrush of the Almighty

Morning clings to the heart with a gentle sun
Embracing the spirit with birdsong and hope
Sensations of creation brought to life by the
Inspirational serenity found within a dawn
Light from above, sent down to stir glory

Peaks and valleys stroke the azure skies
With heavenly insights discovered in truth
Inspired by soft teardrops lingering inside
The one who knows the power of this promise
Coloring the mountains' hues of blue and purple

REGINA McINTOSH

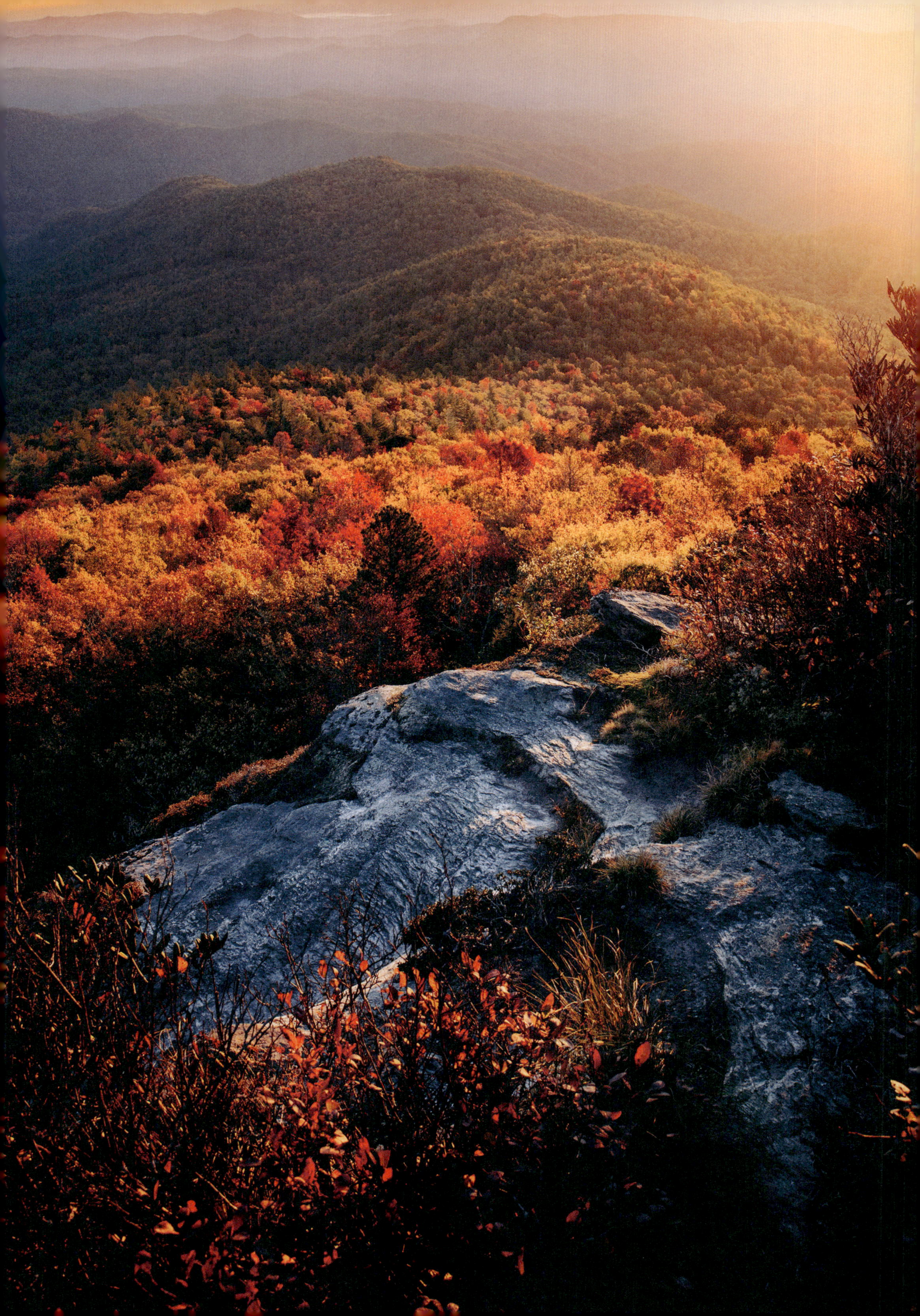

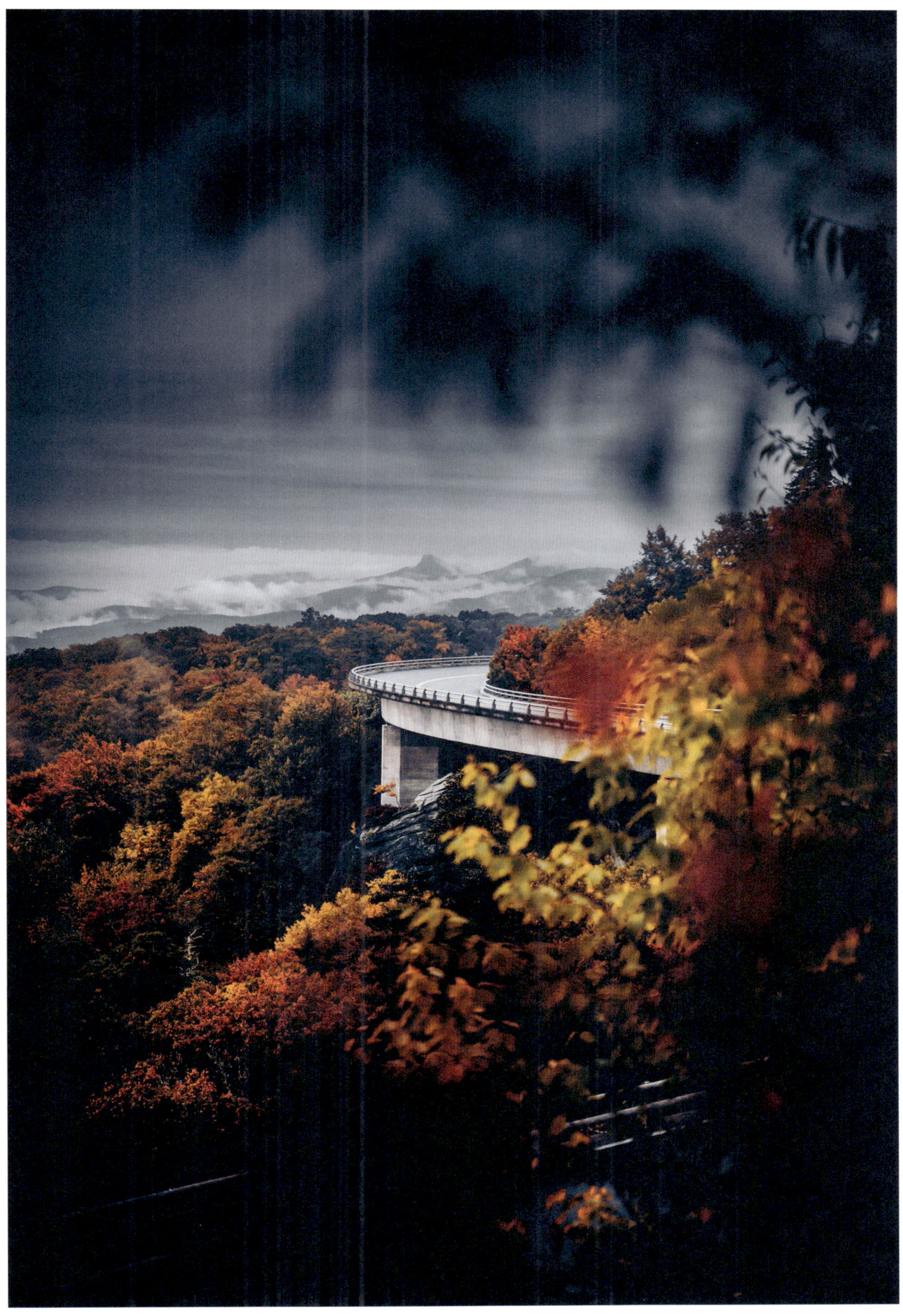

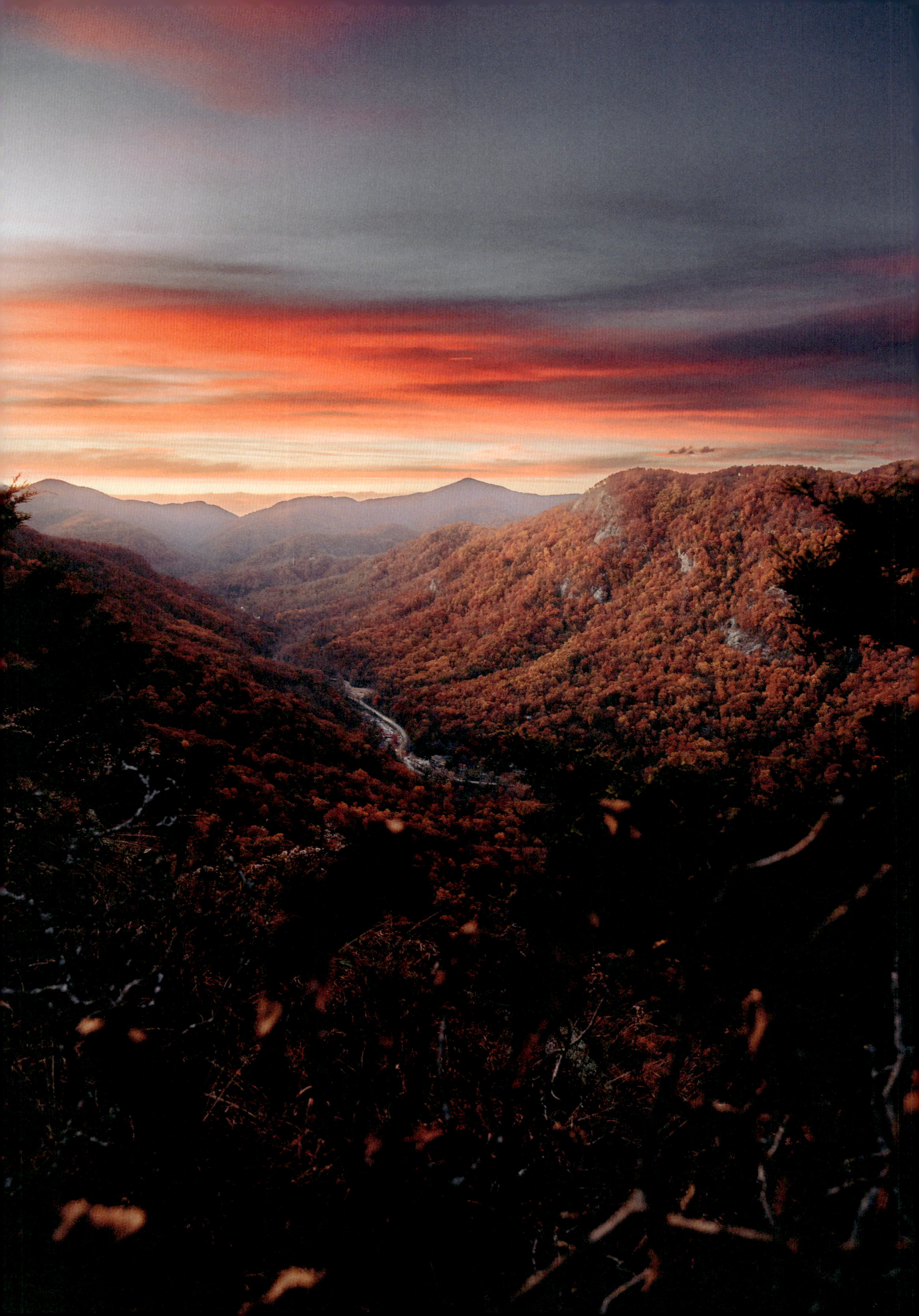

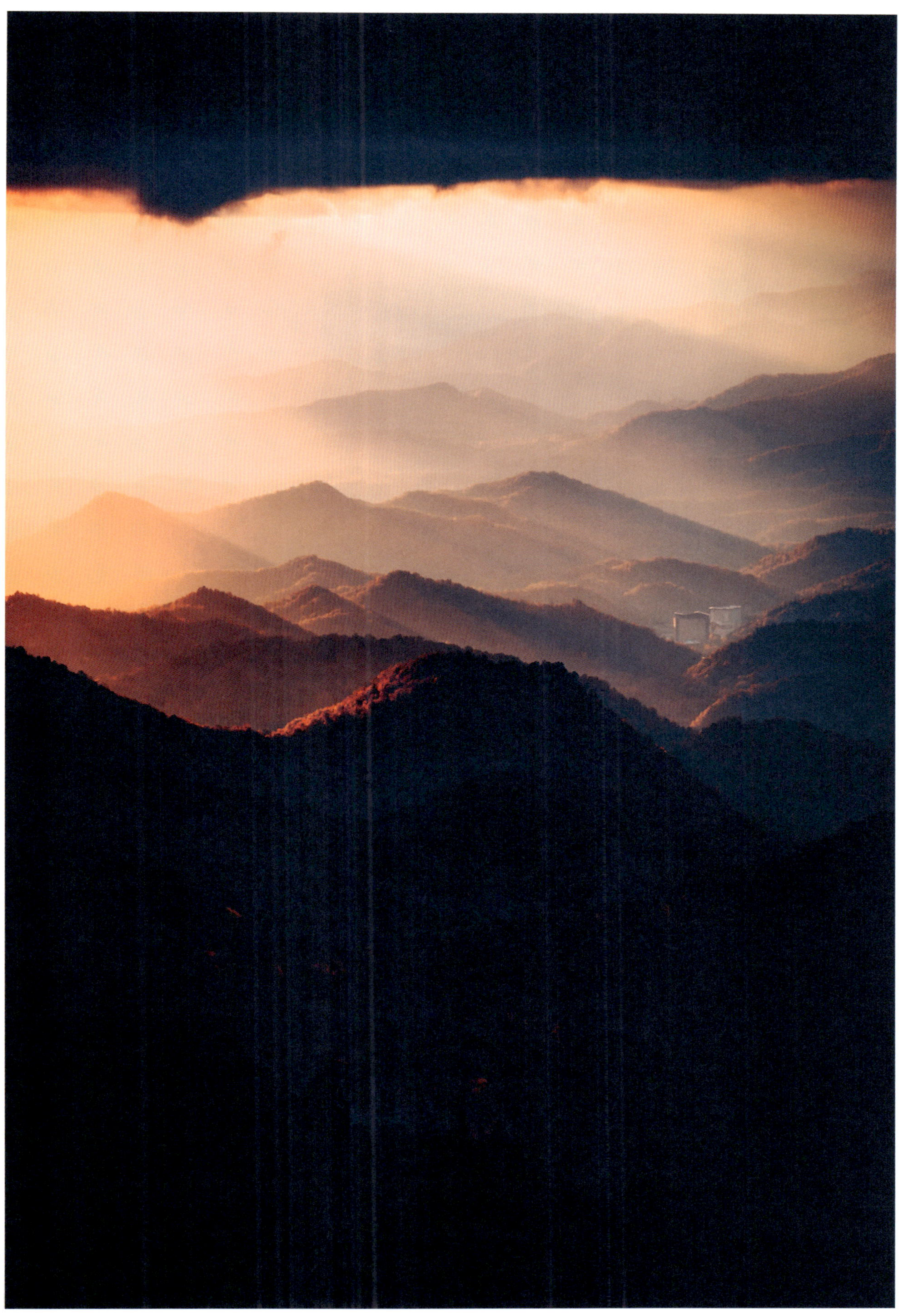

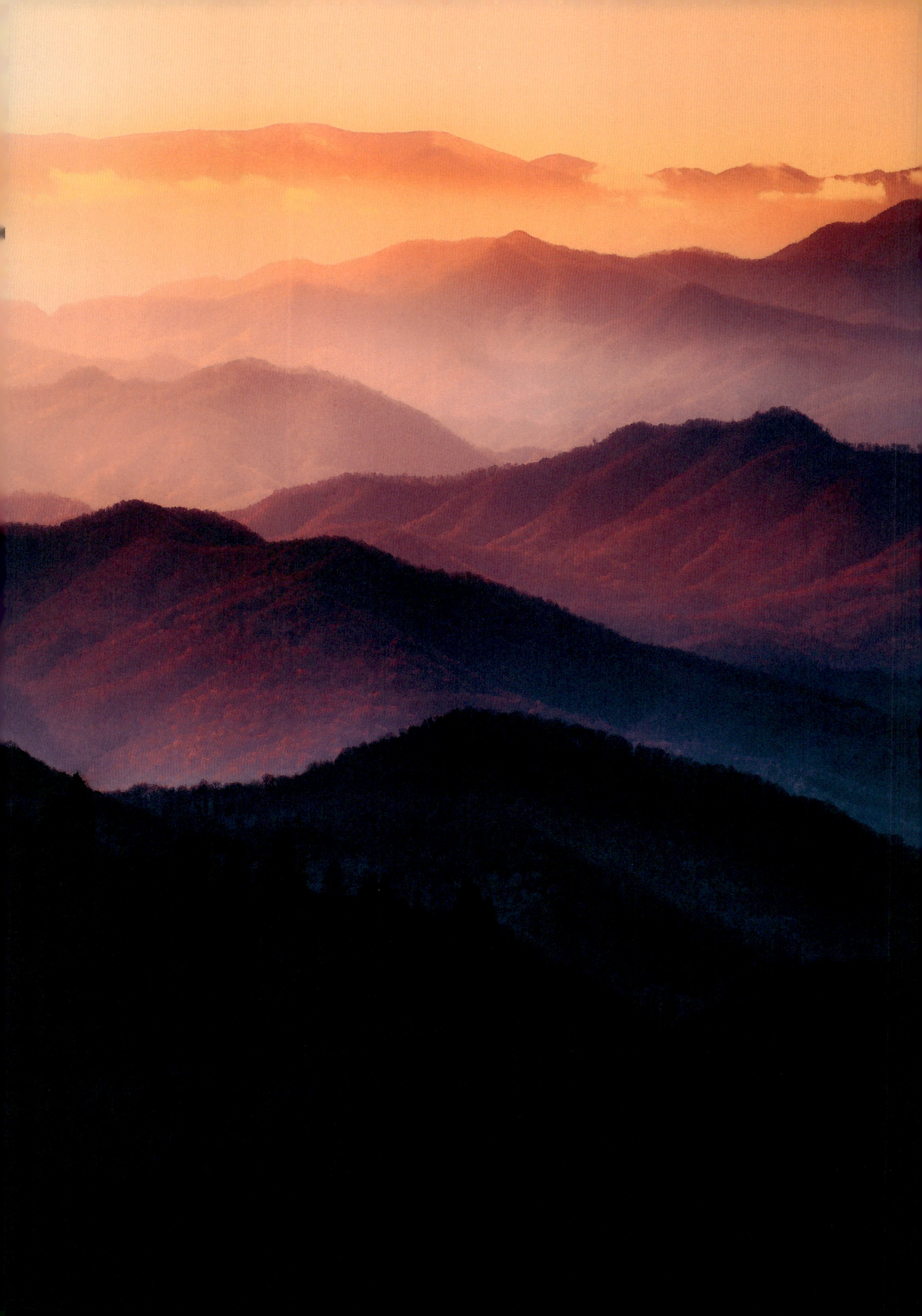

Memories made in
the mountains stay
in our hearts forever.

ANONYMOUS

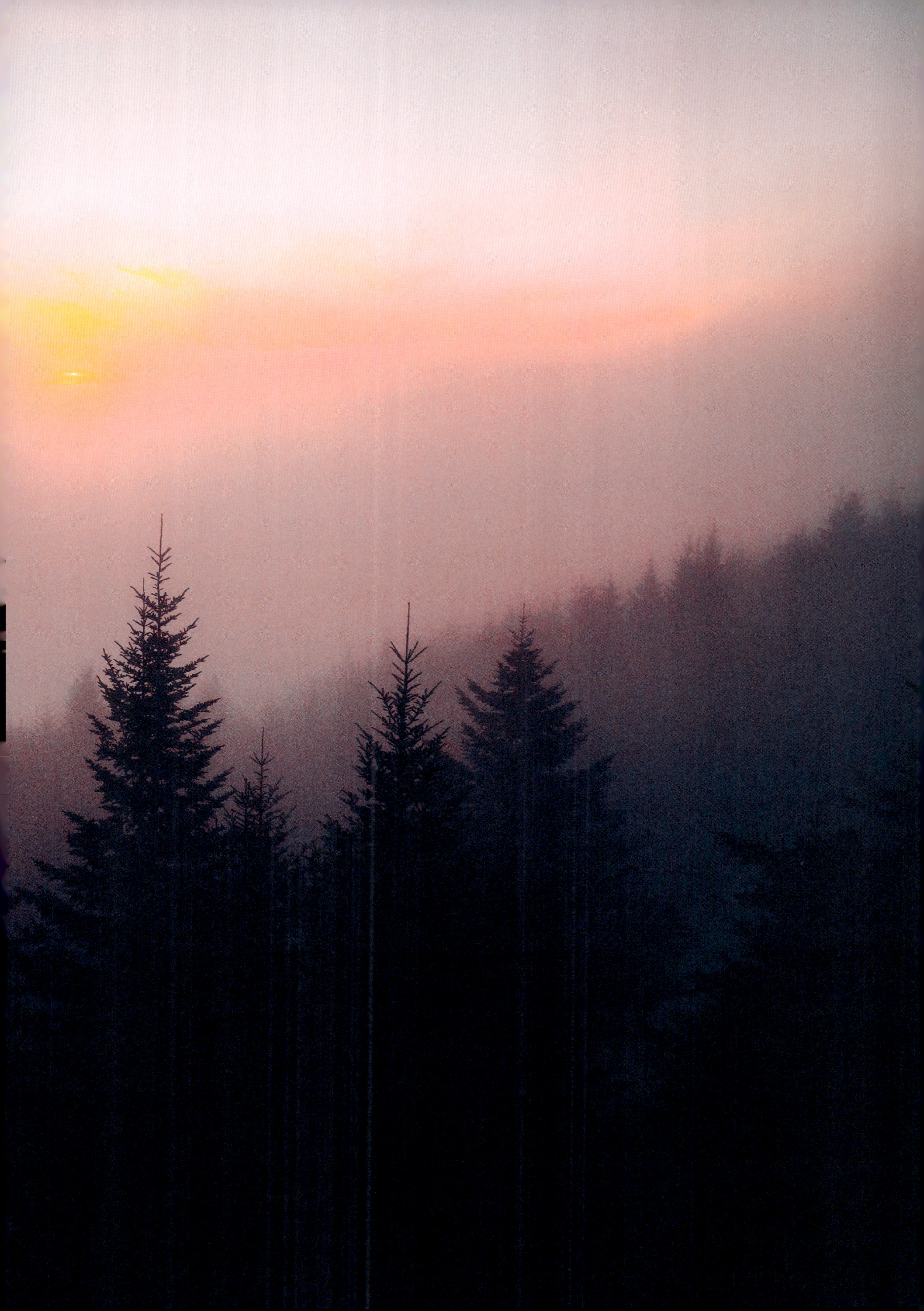

Blue Ridge Mountains

Sometimes I am in doubt
about why I am here

Here amongst these mountains
certainly not just anywhere

The path seemed to just effortlessly
want to open itself to me

The draw was powerfully magnetic
So I surrendered and let go
of the part that was hectic

Often now as I drive over a hill
and I look into a luscious green dale
my feelings of joy give me little chills

My eyes water and my breath is taken away
by the beauty I am surrounded by
every single day.

WILLOW LAWRENCE

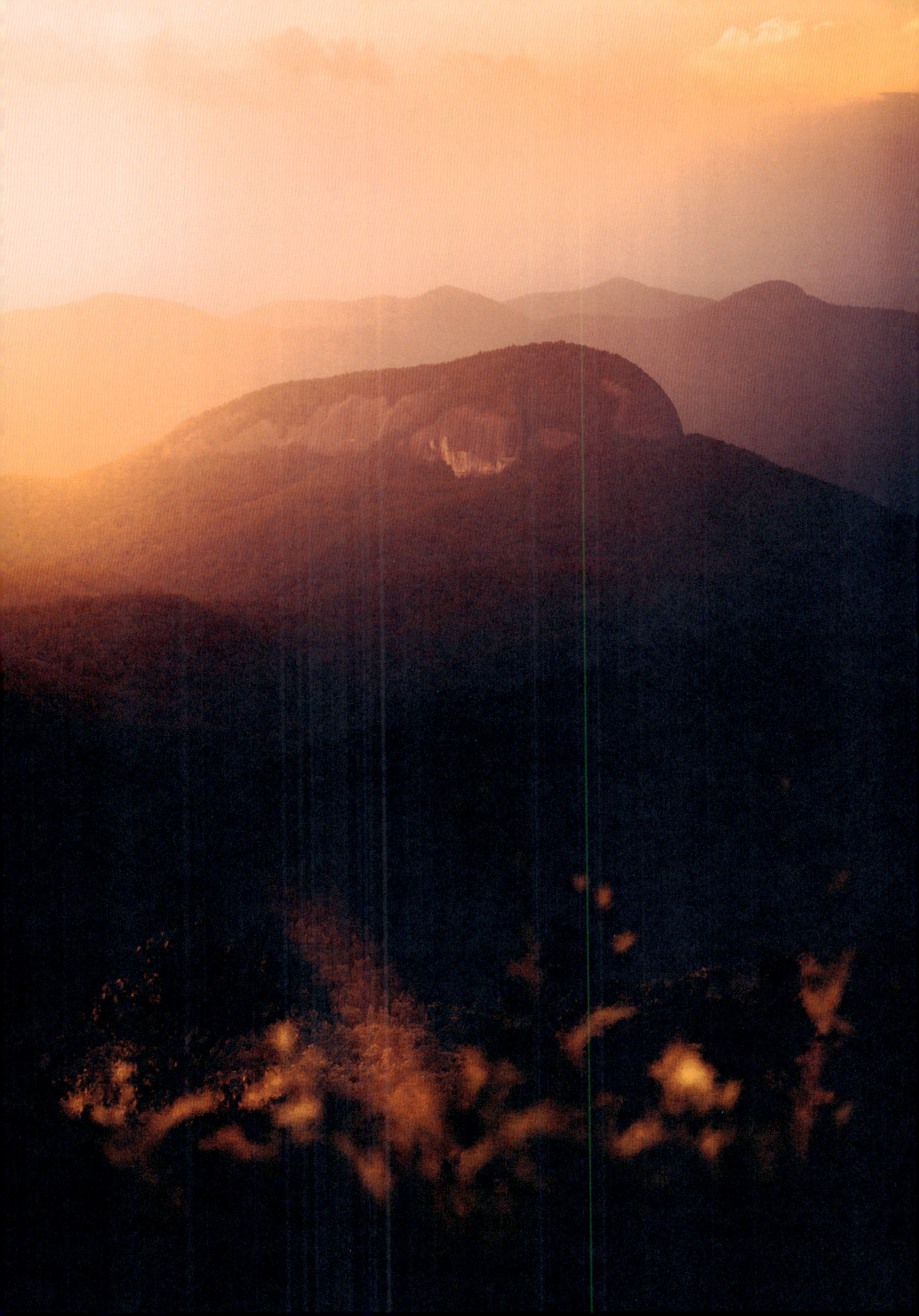

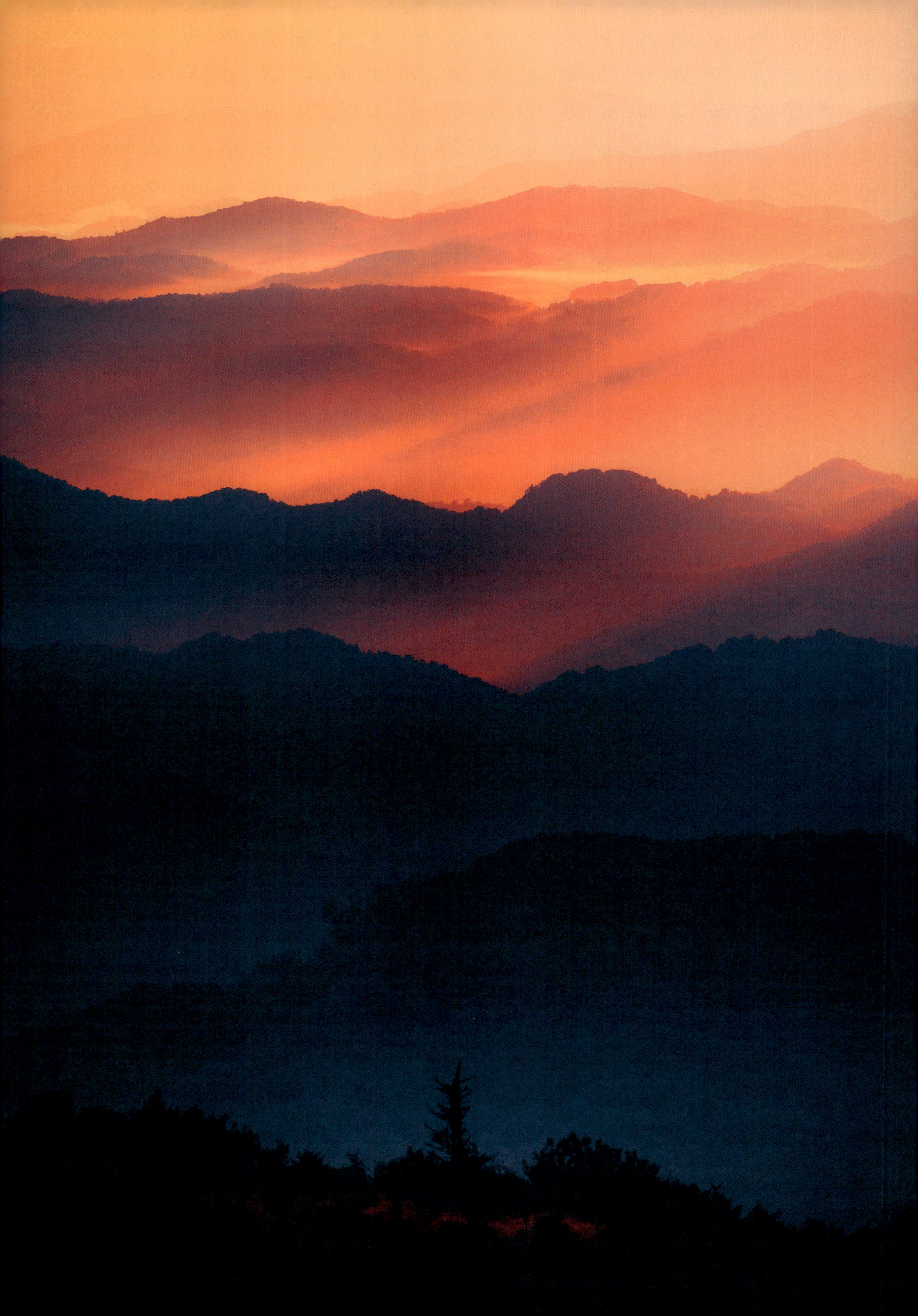

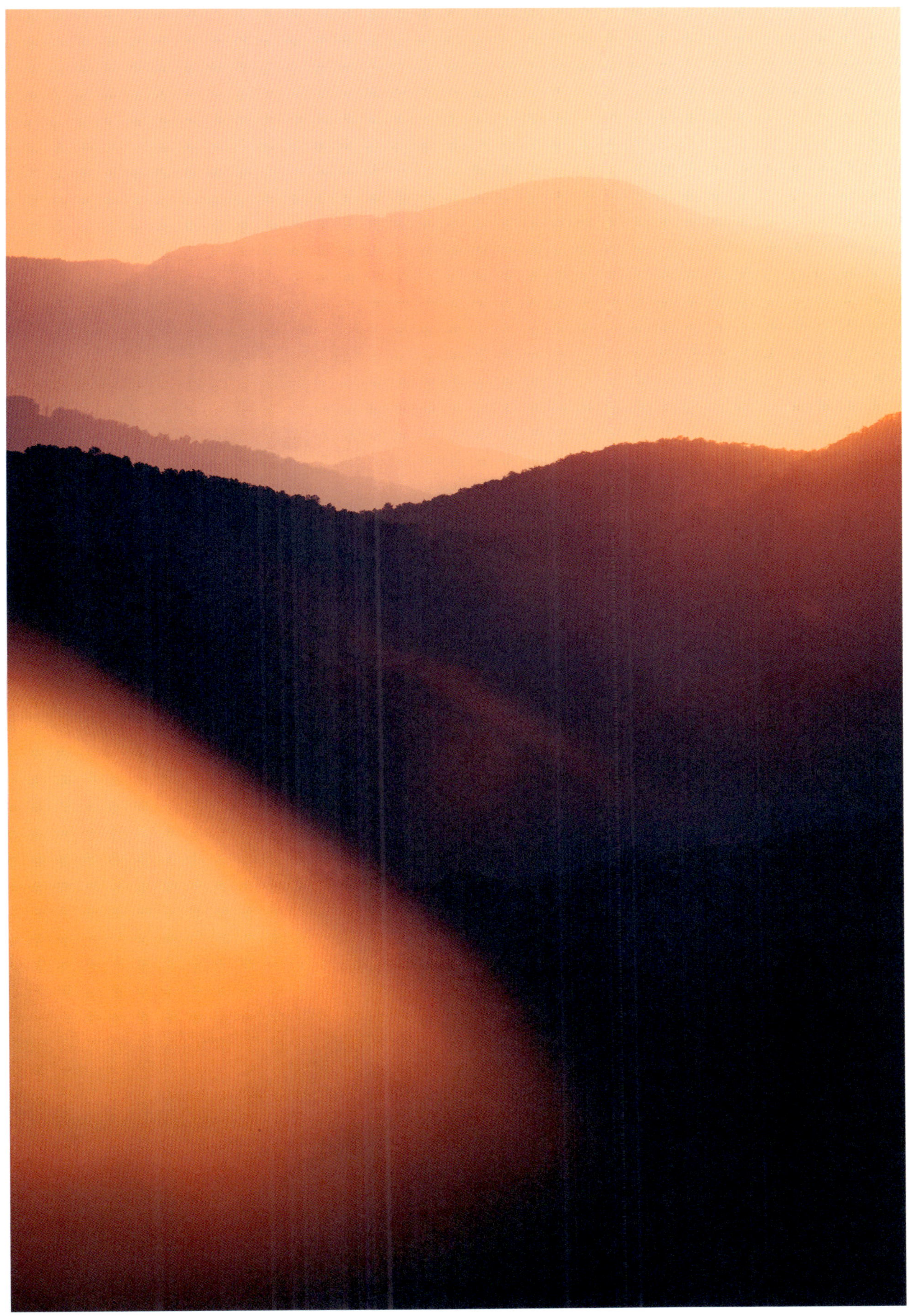

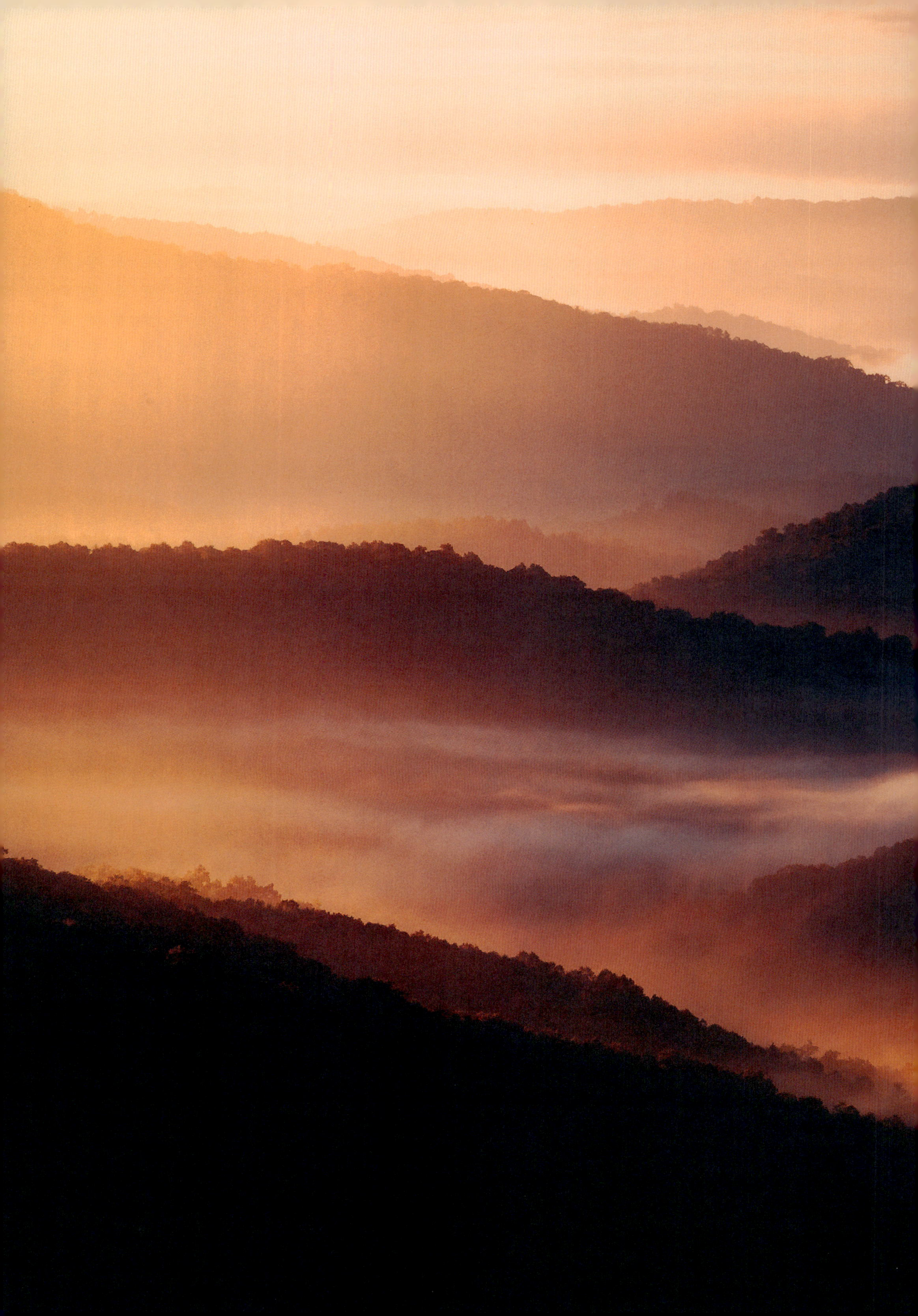

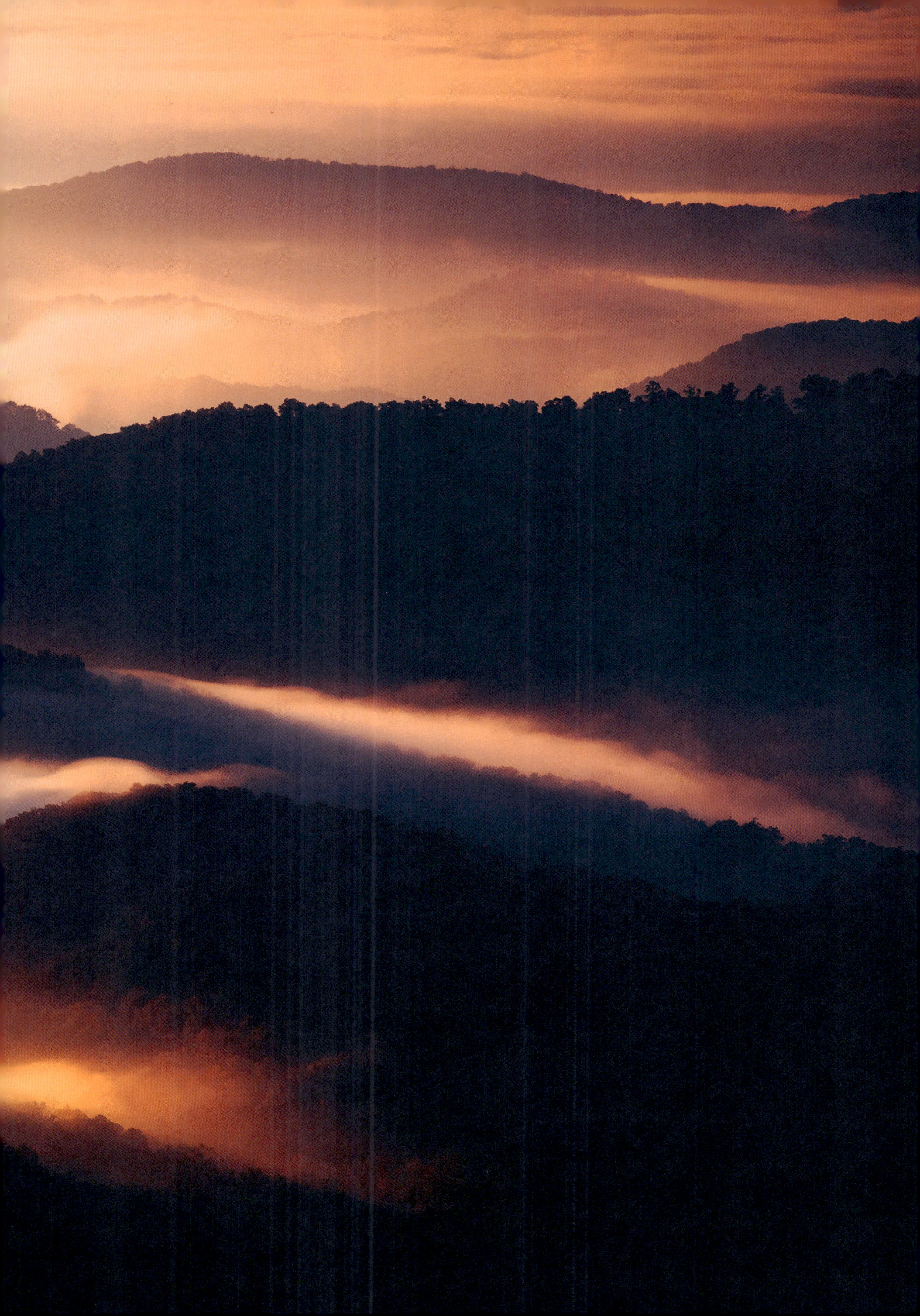

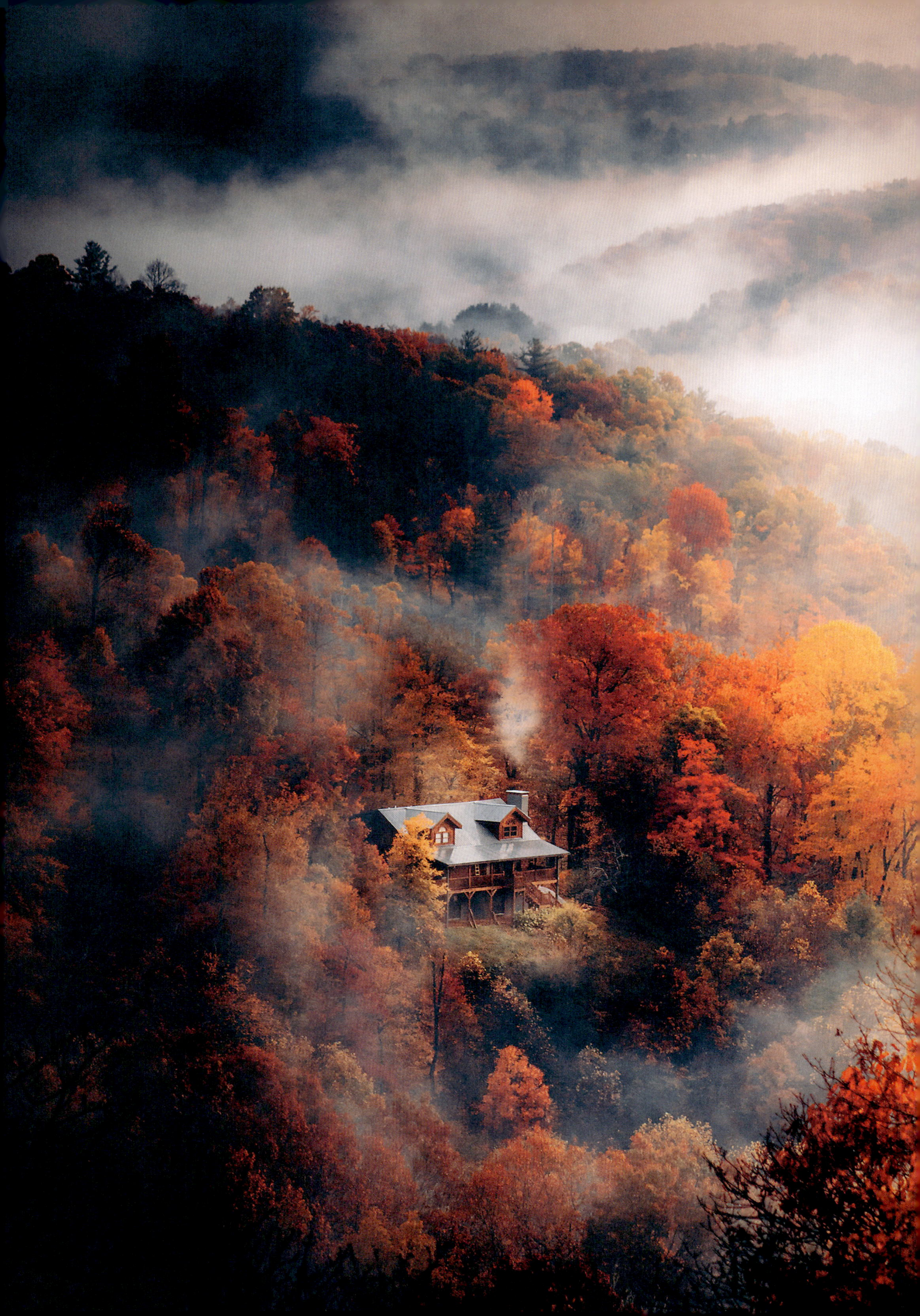

Adopt the pace of nature:
her secret is patience.

RALPH WALDO EMERSON

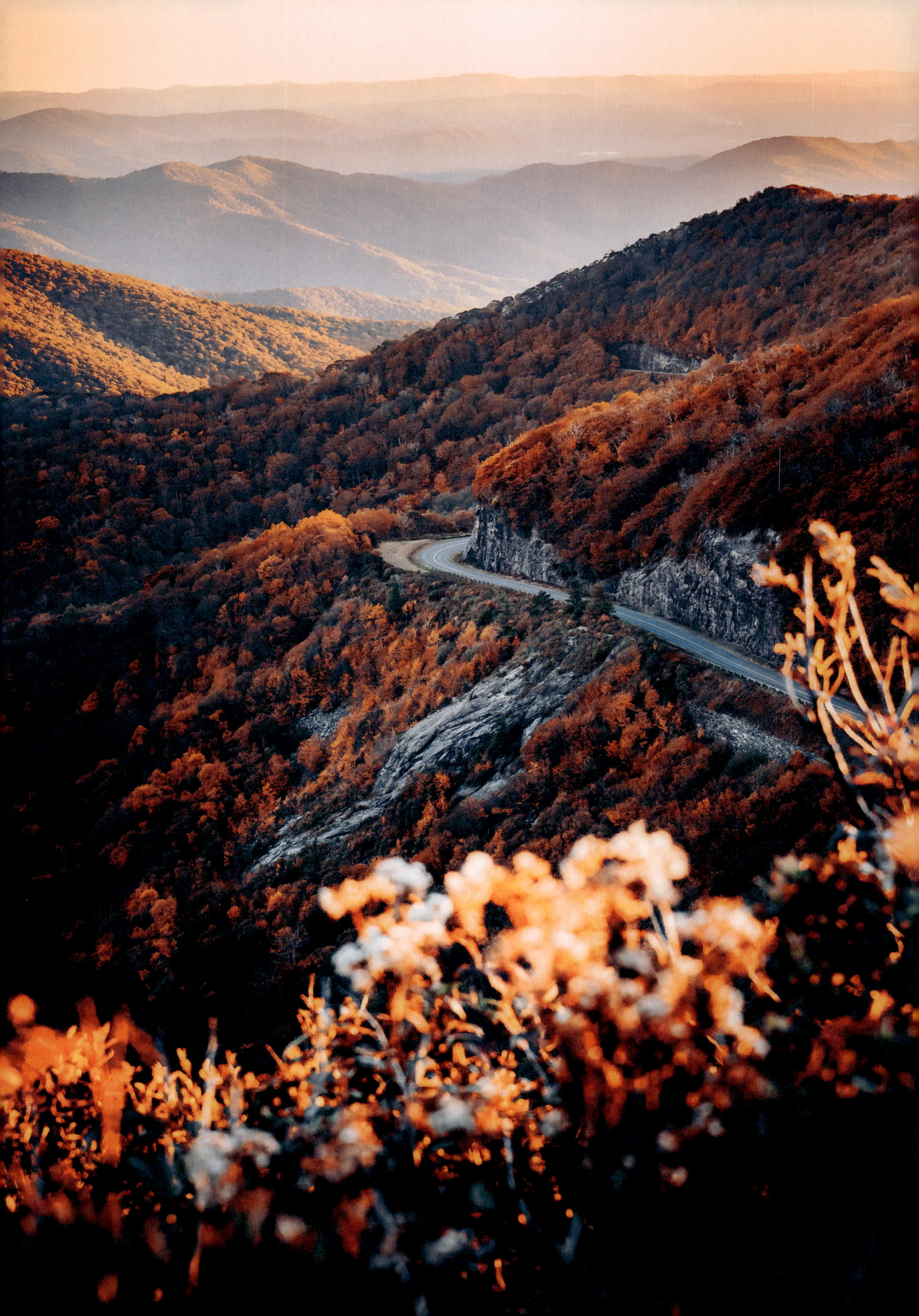

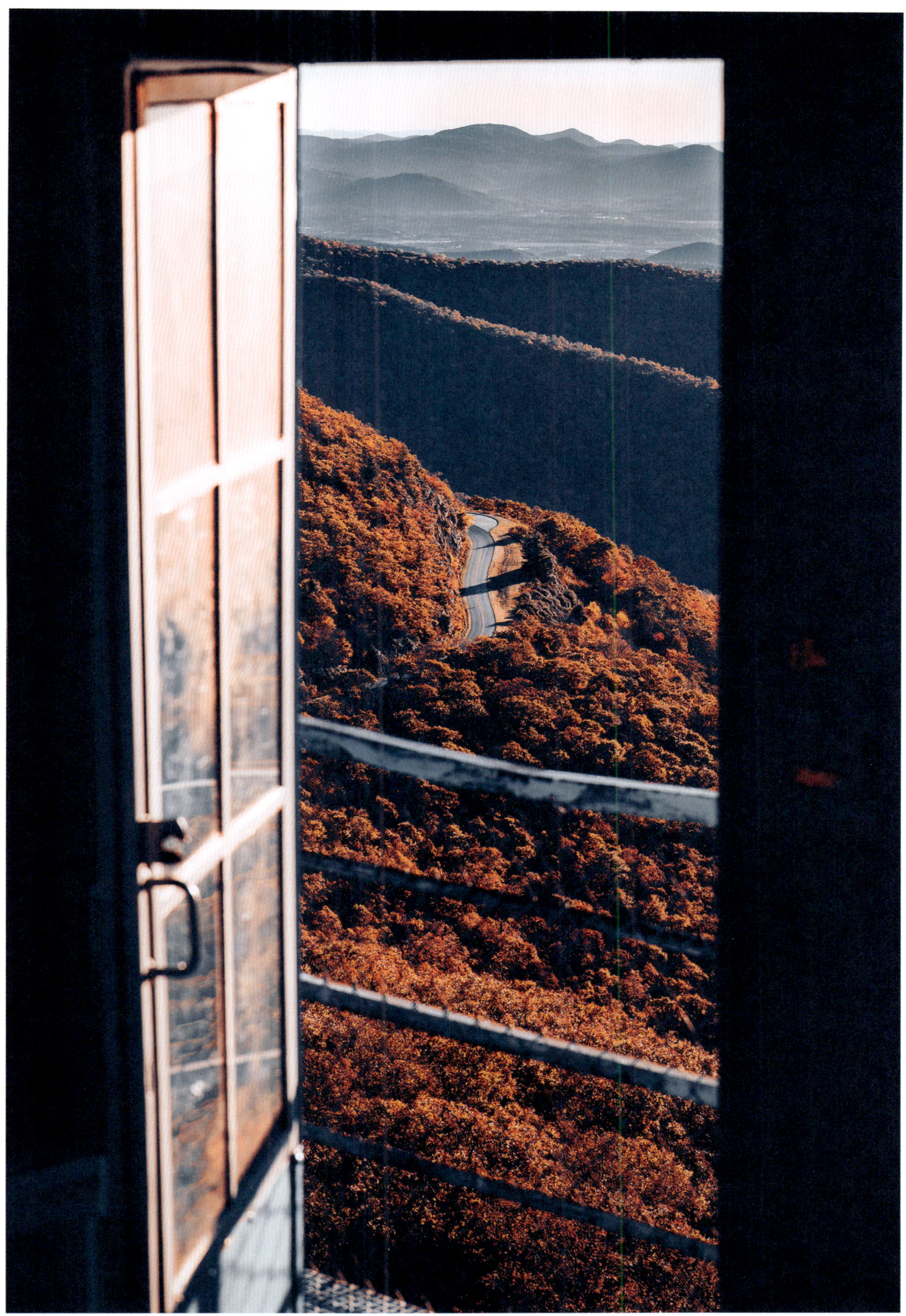

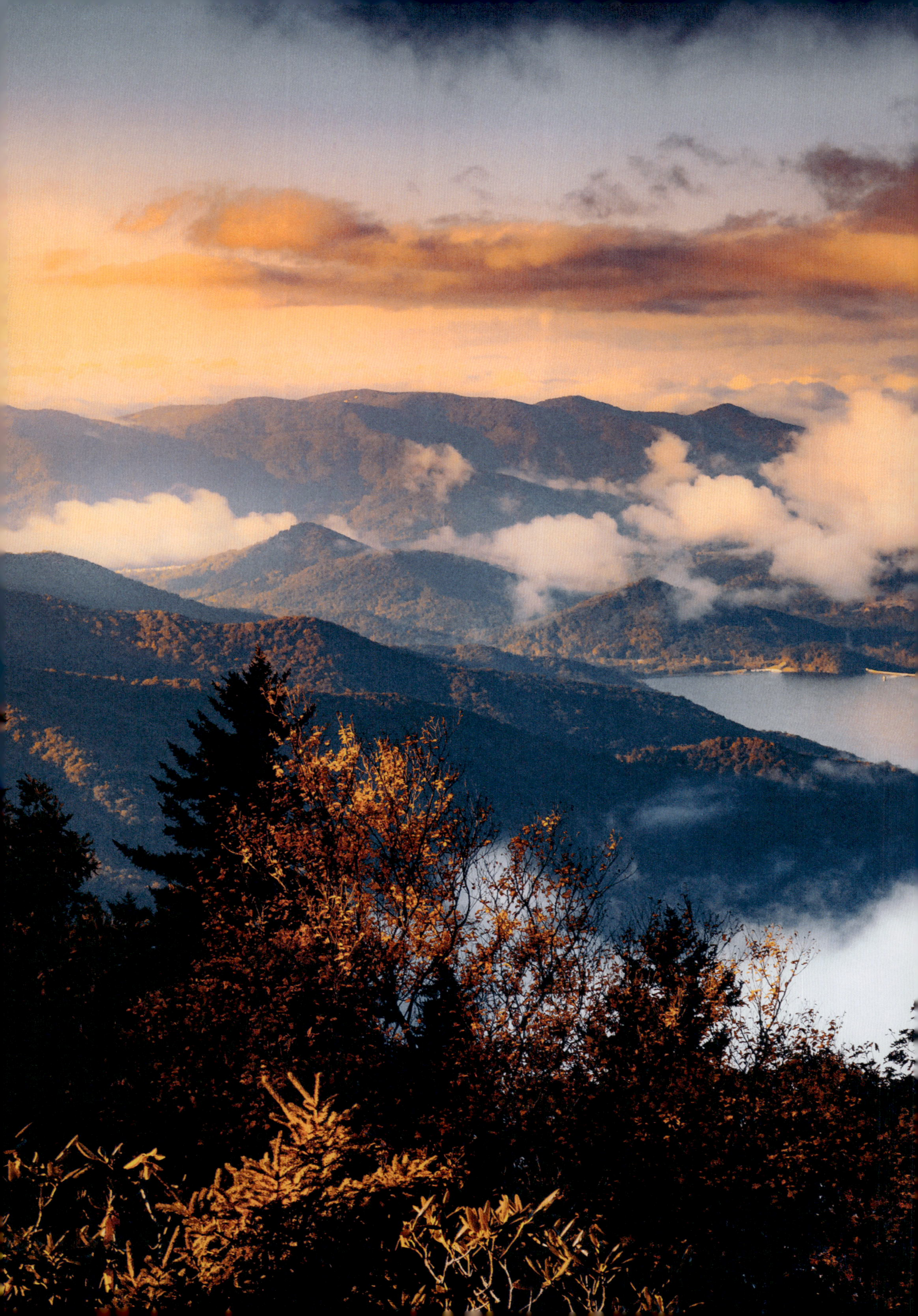

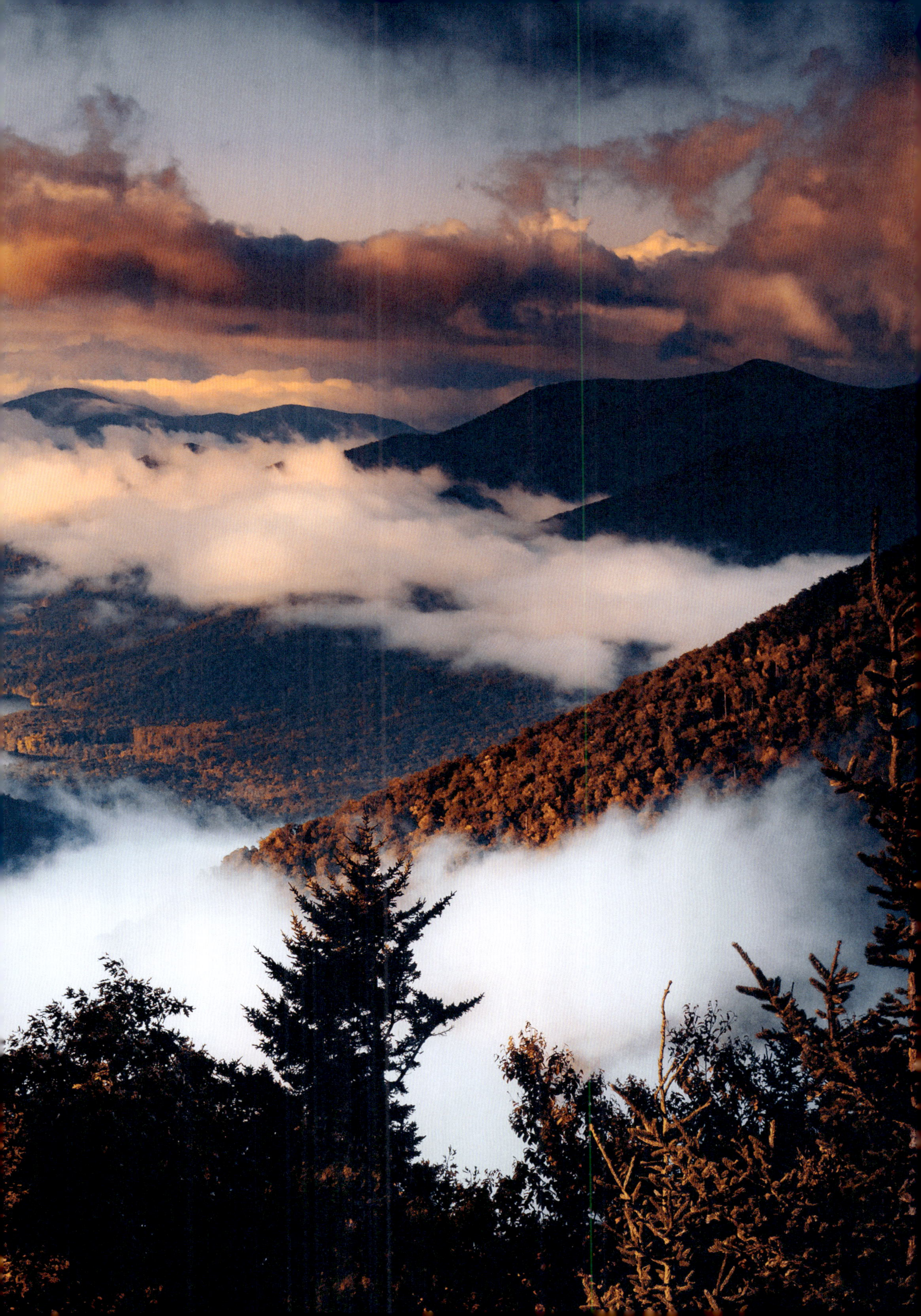

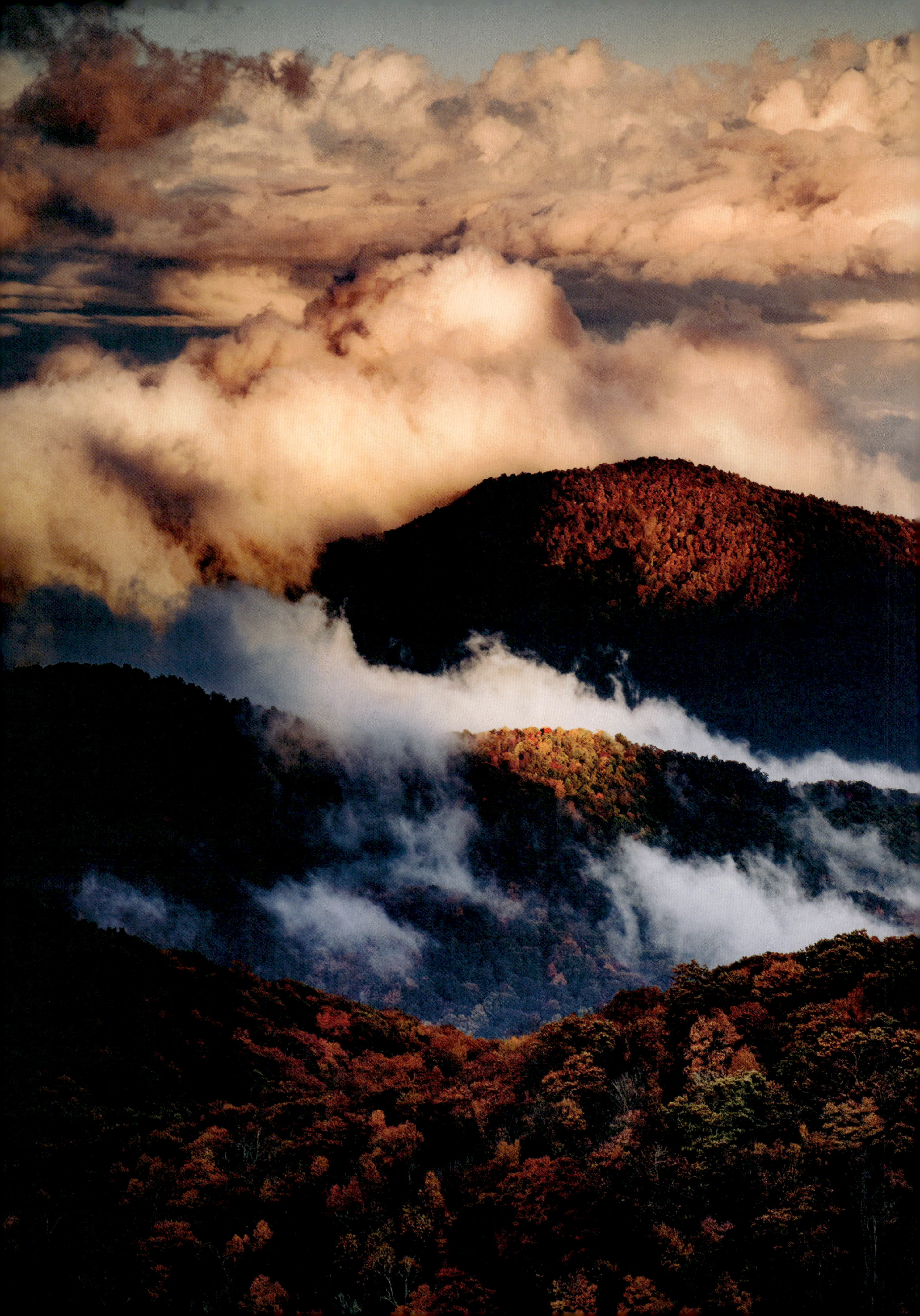

In the mountains,
there you feel free.

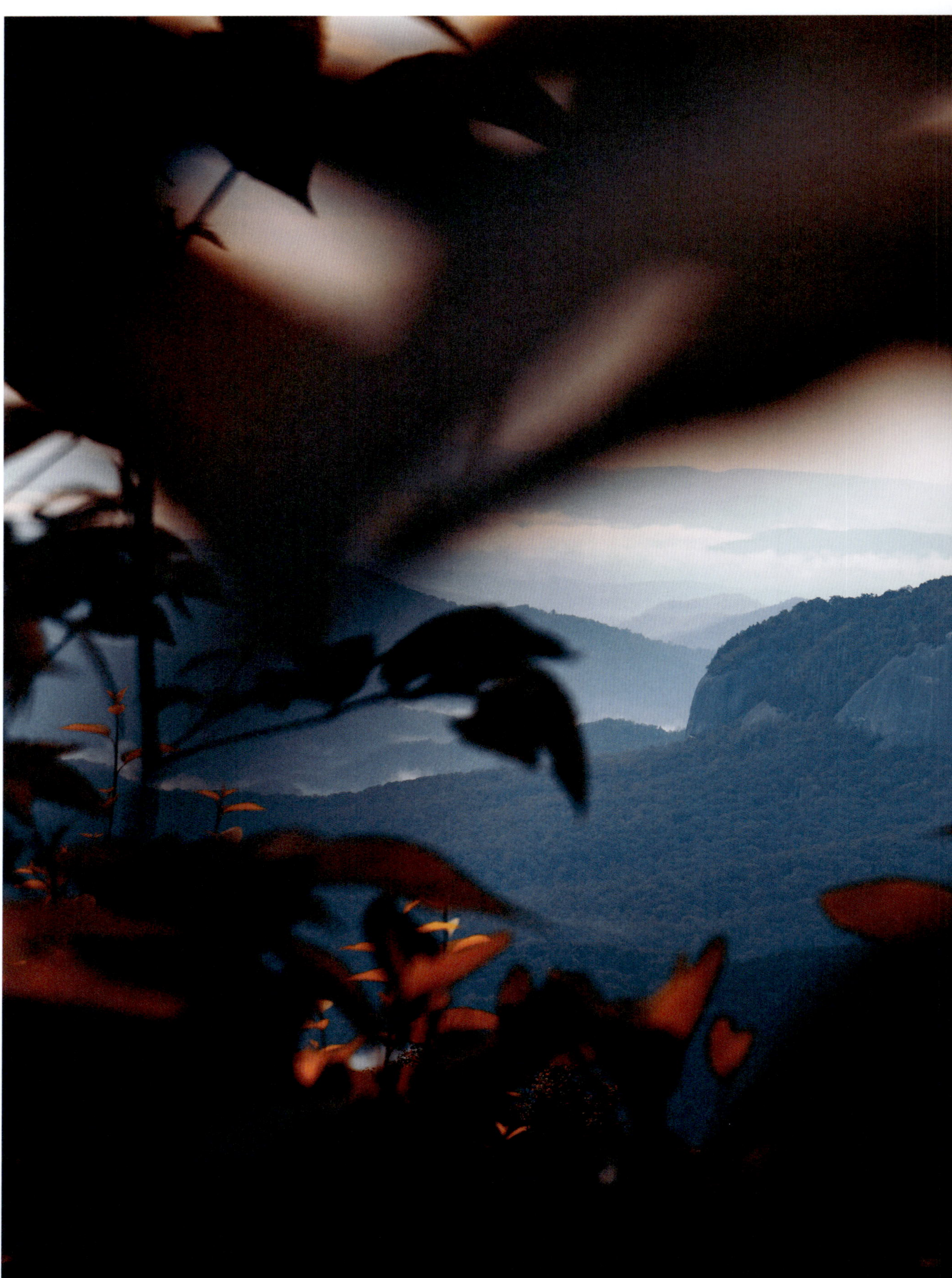

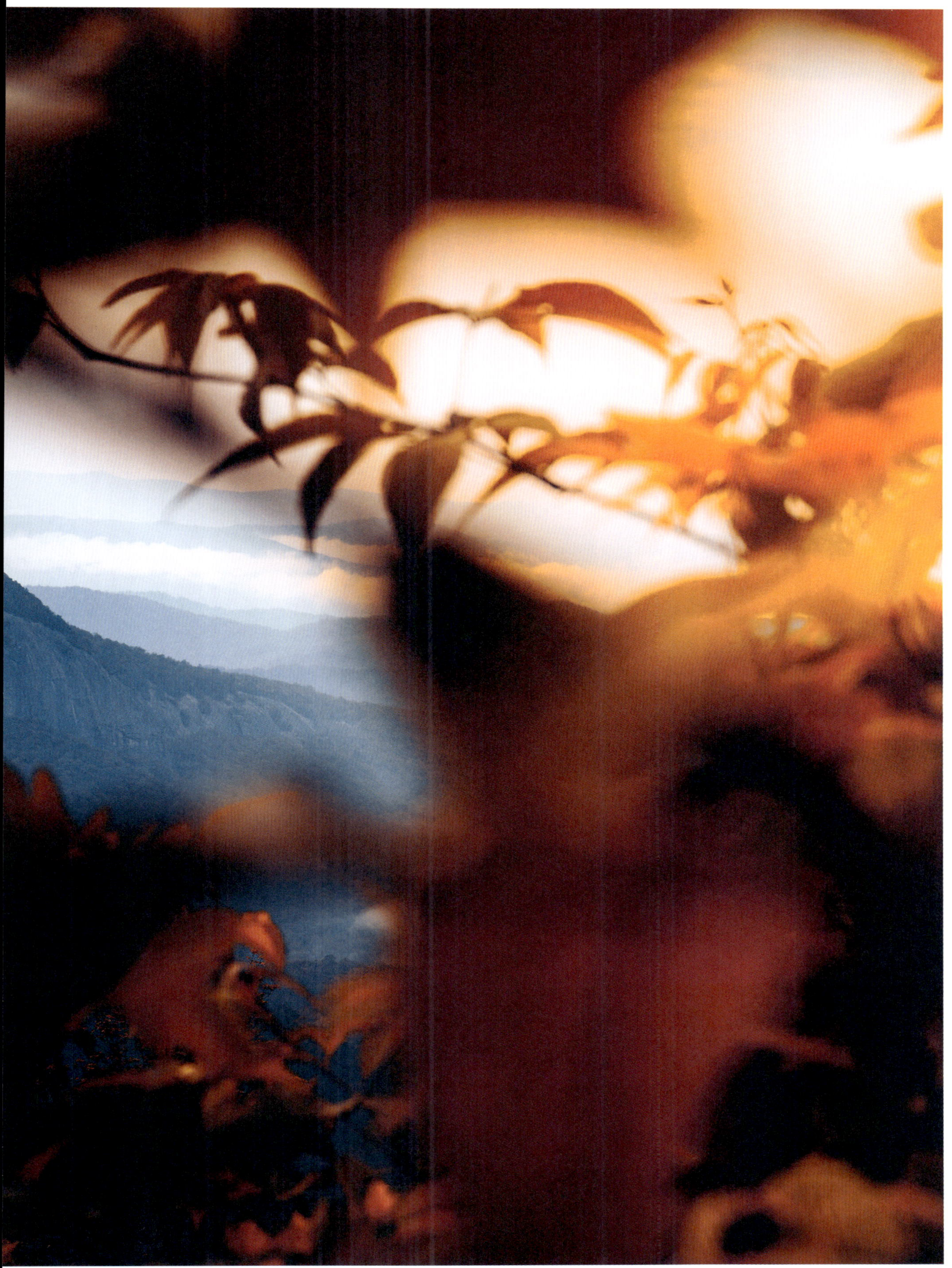

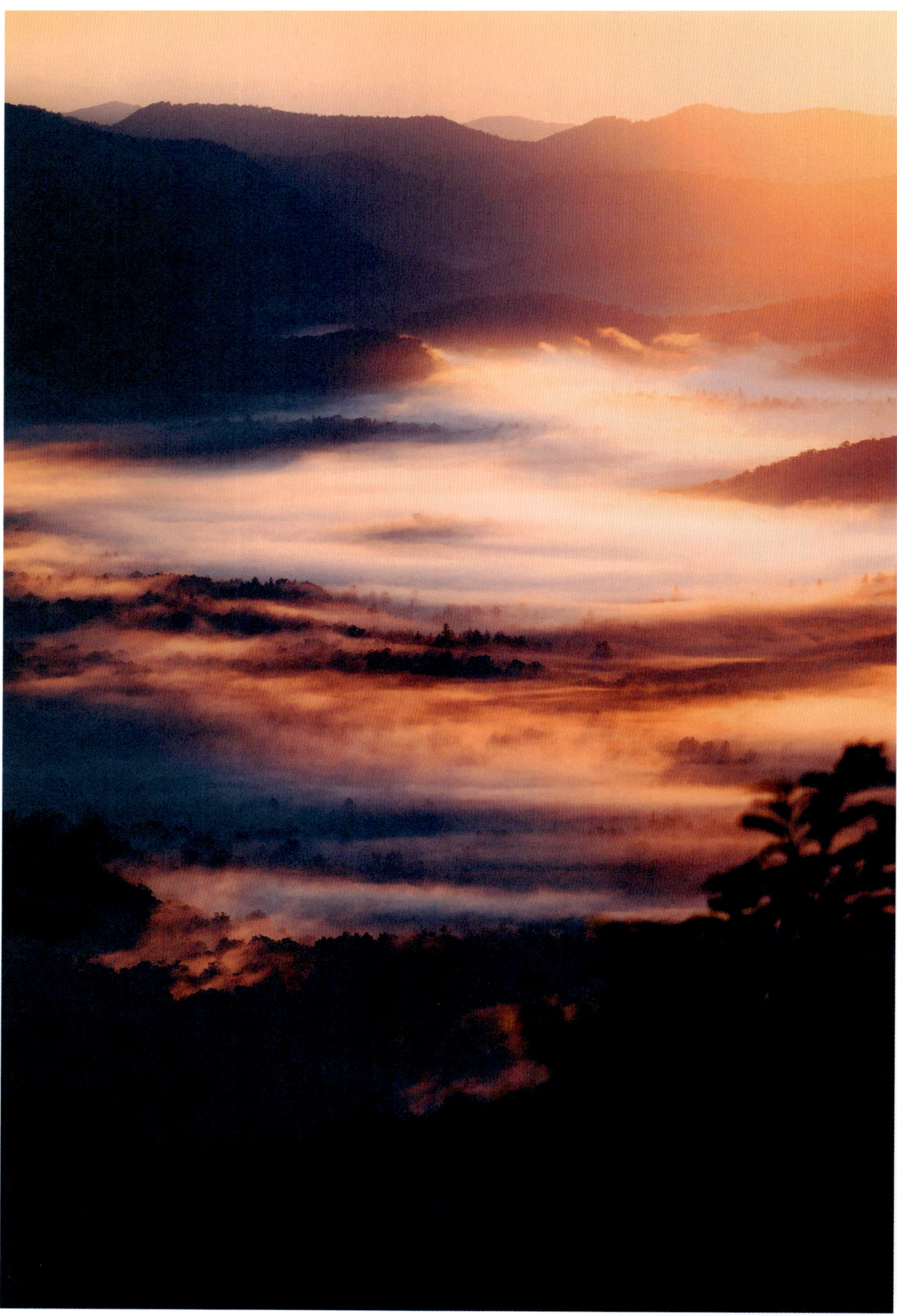

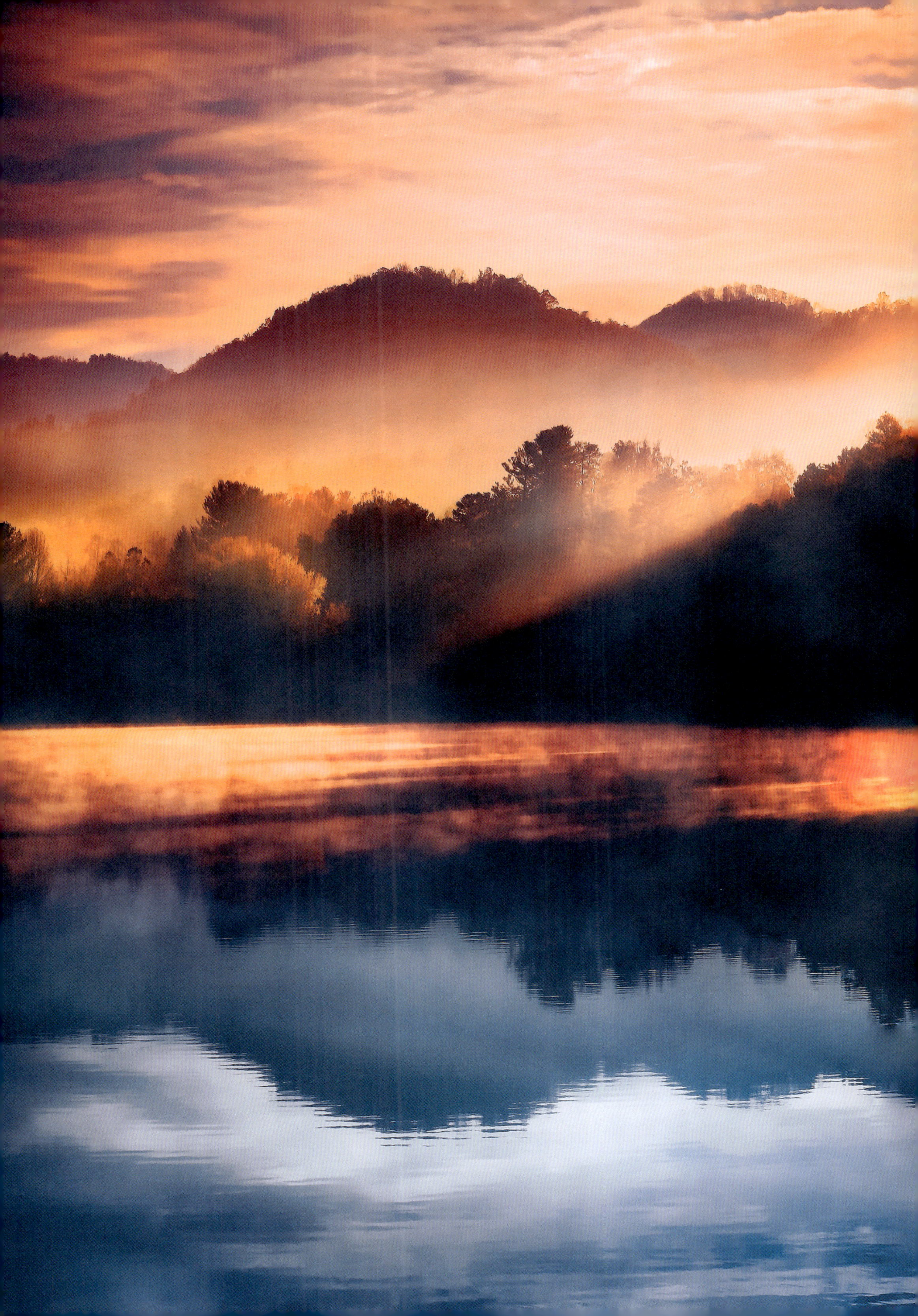

Clouds

Over the high ridge
clouds blossom
from an emptiness
of flame-blue sky,
blossom and vanish
and blossom and vanish again
in a display
of planetary
prestidigitation.

RICHARD GREENE

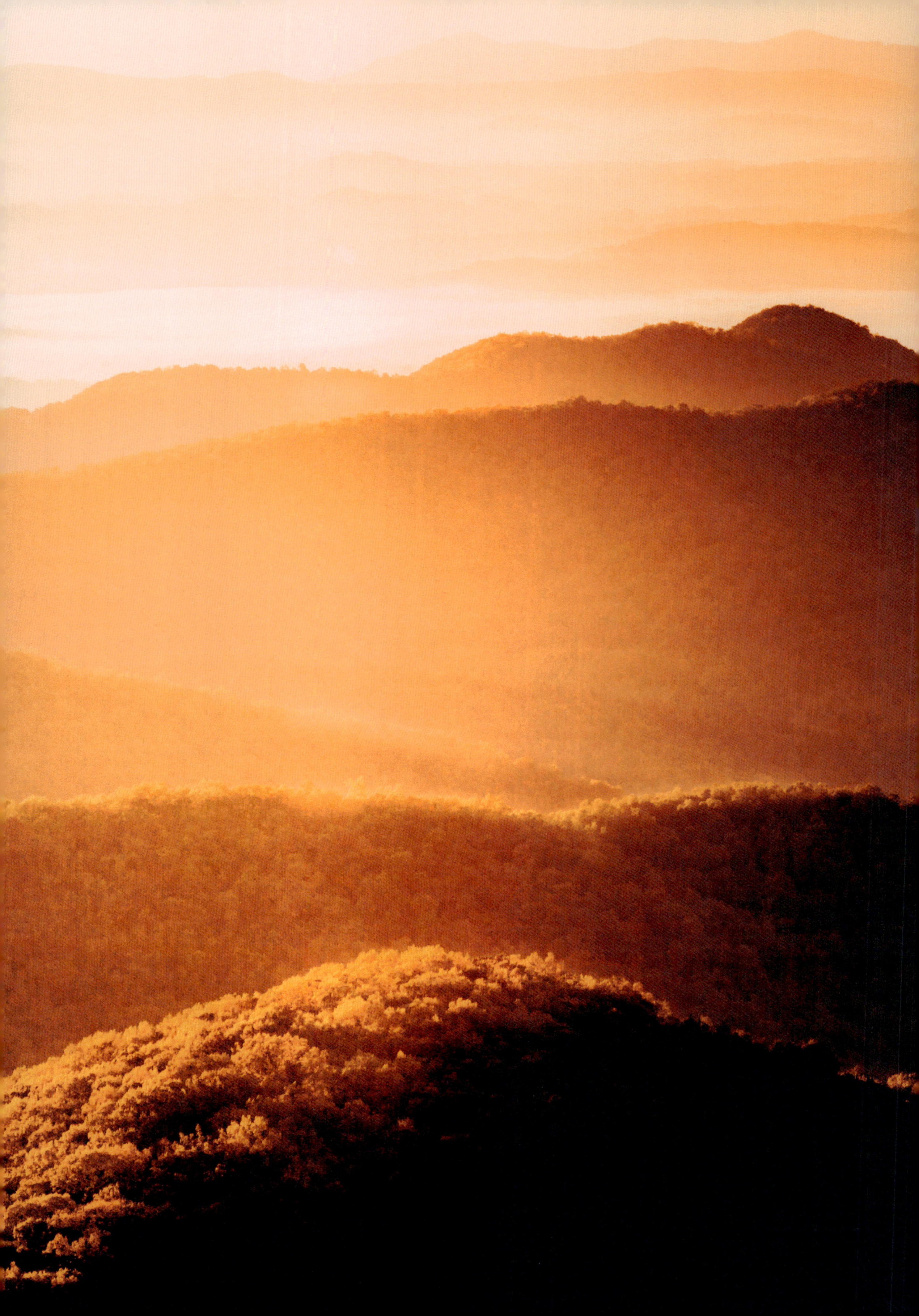

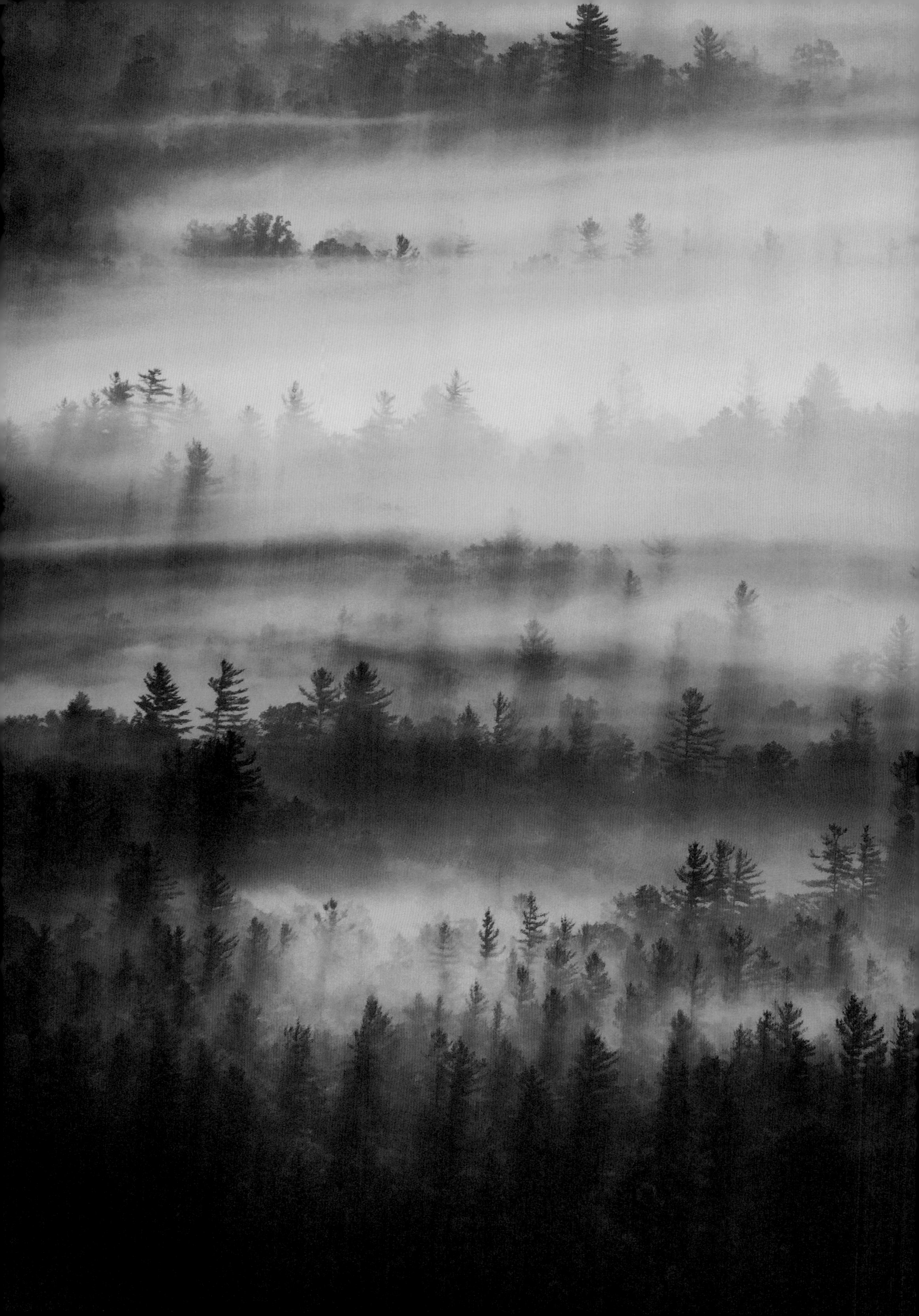

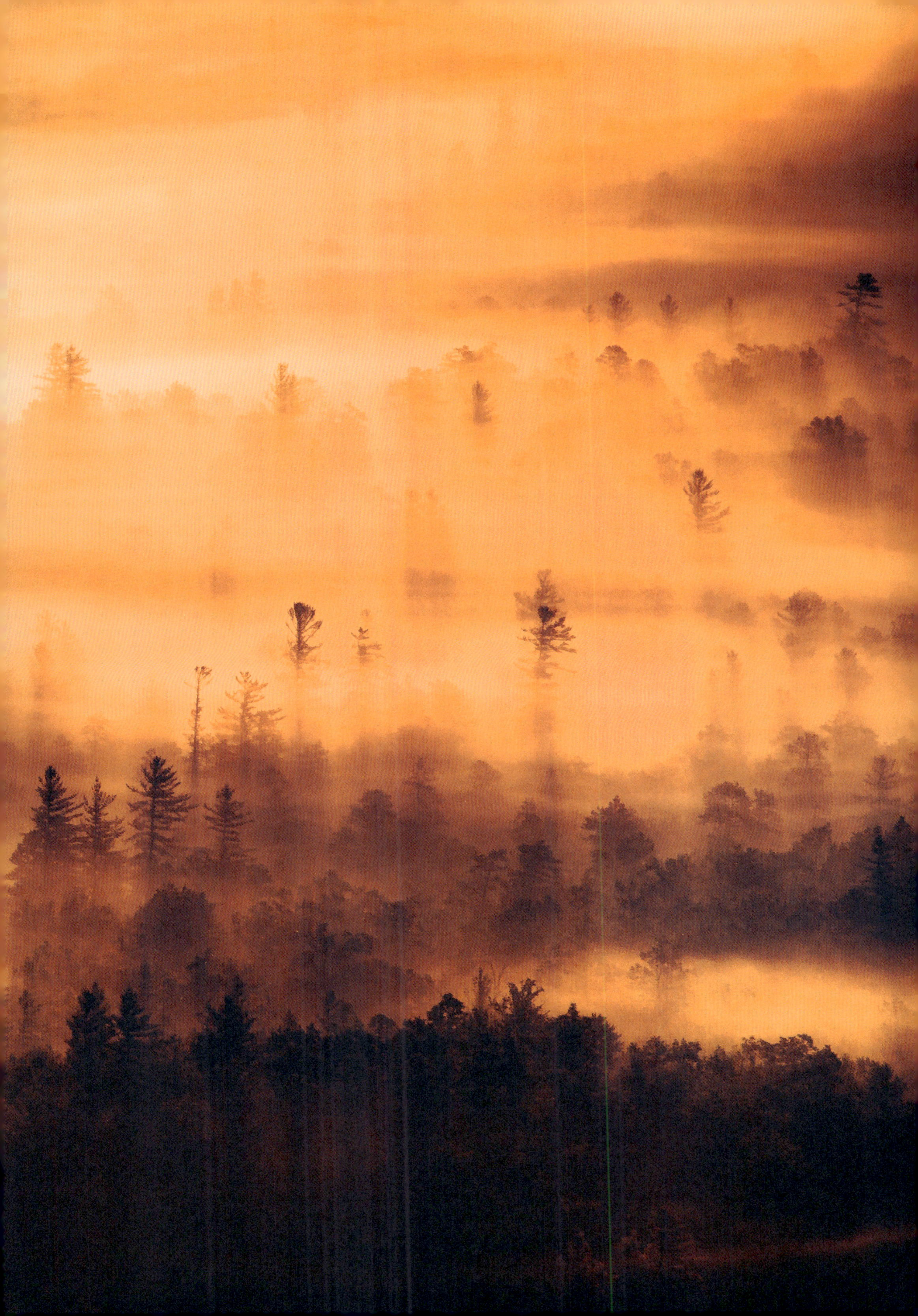

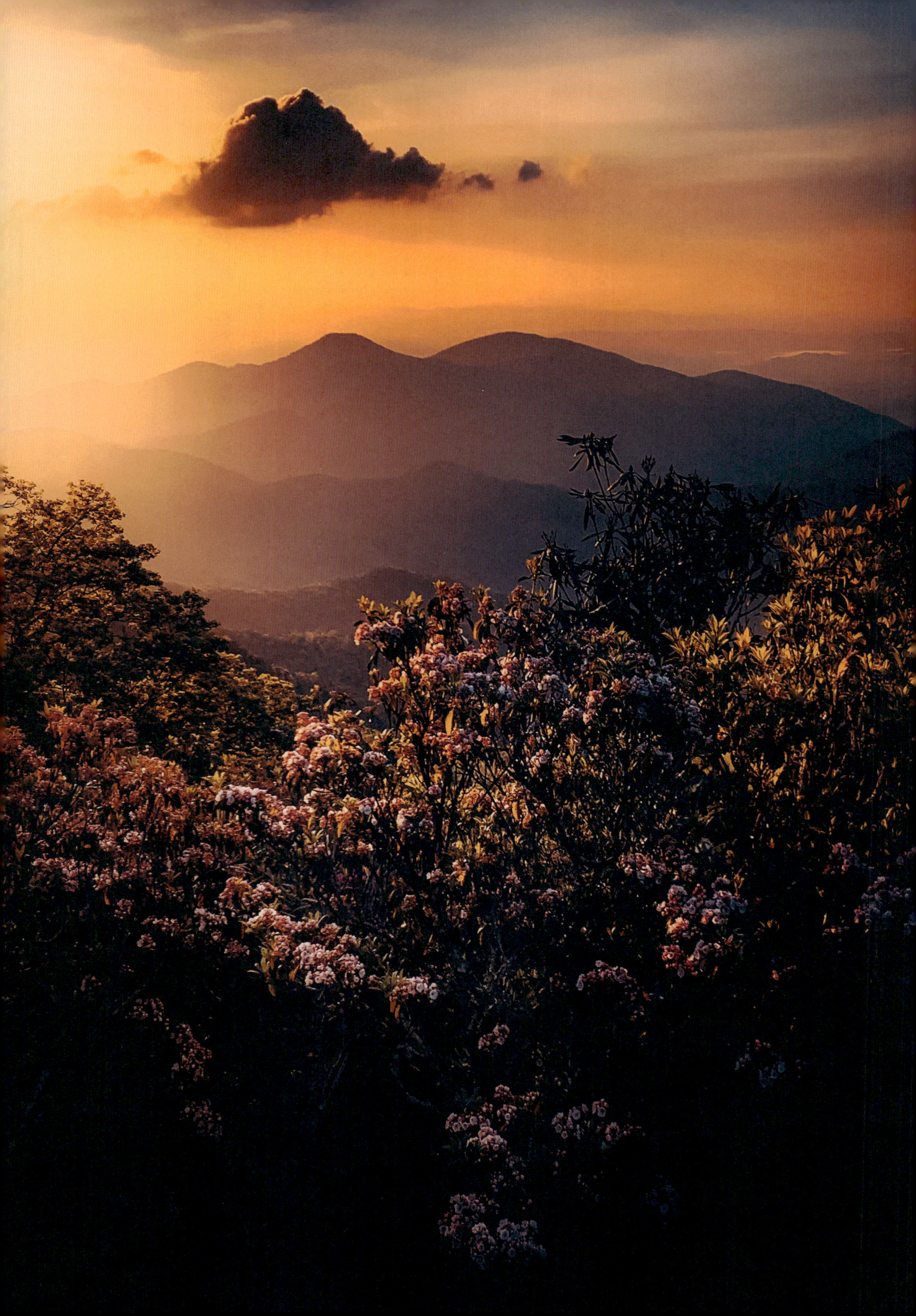

Nature does not
hurry, yet everything
is accomplished.

LAO TZU

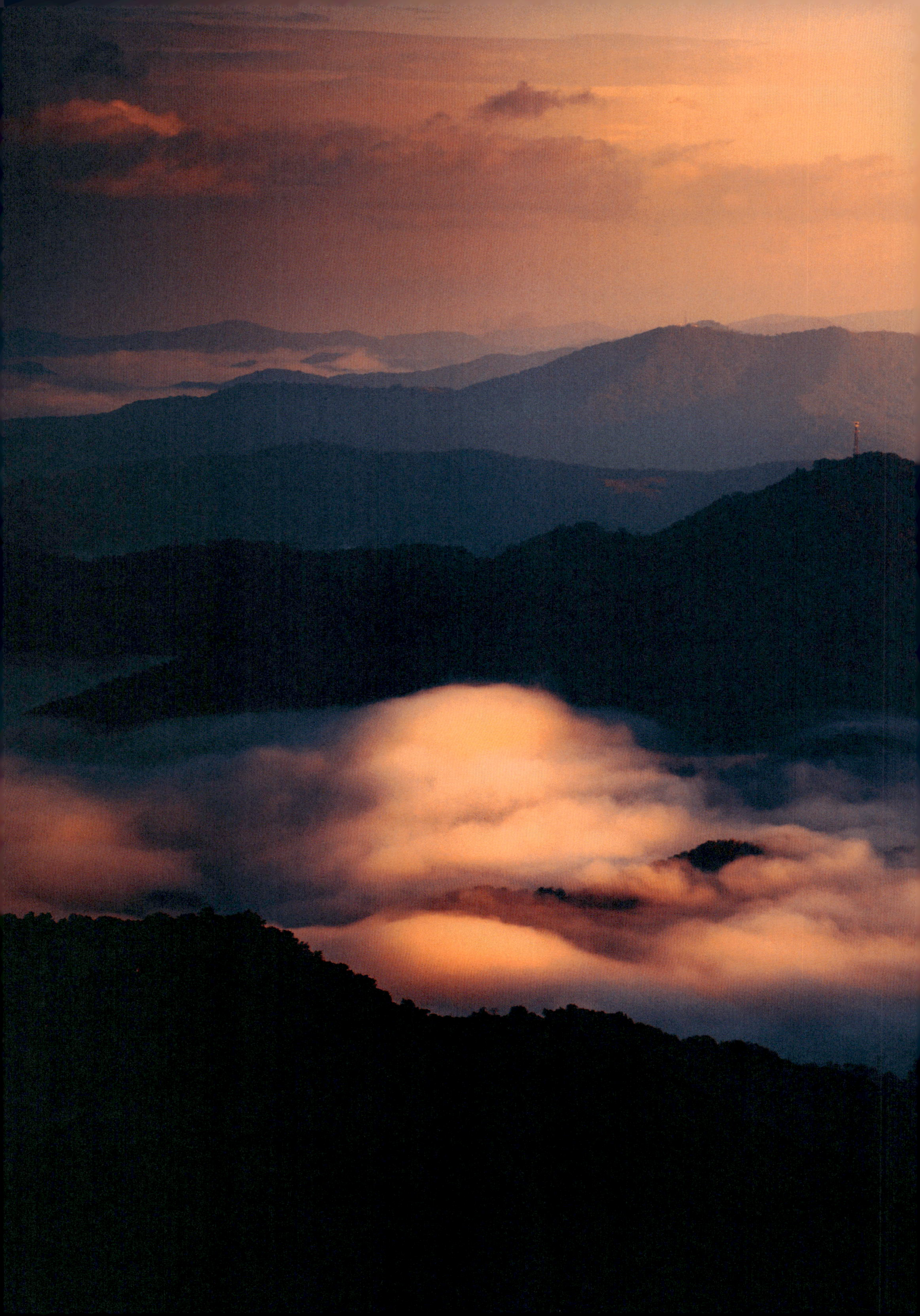

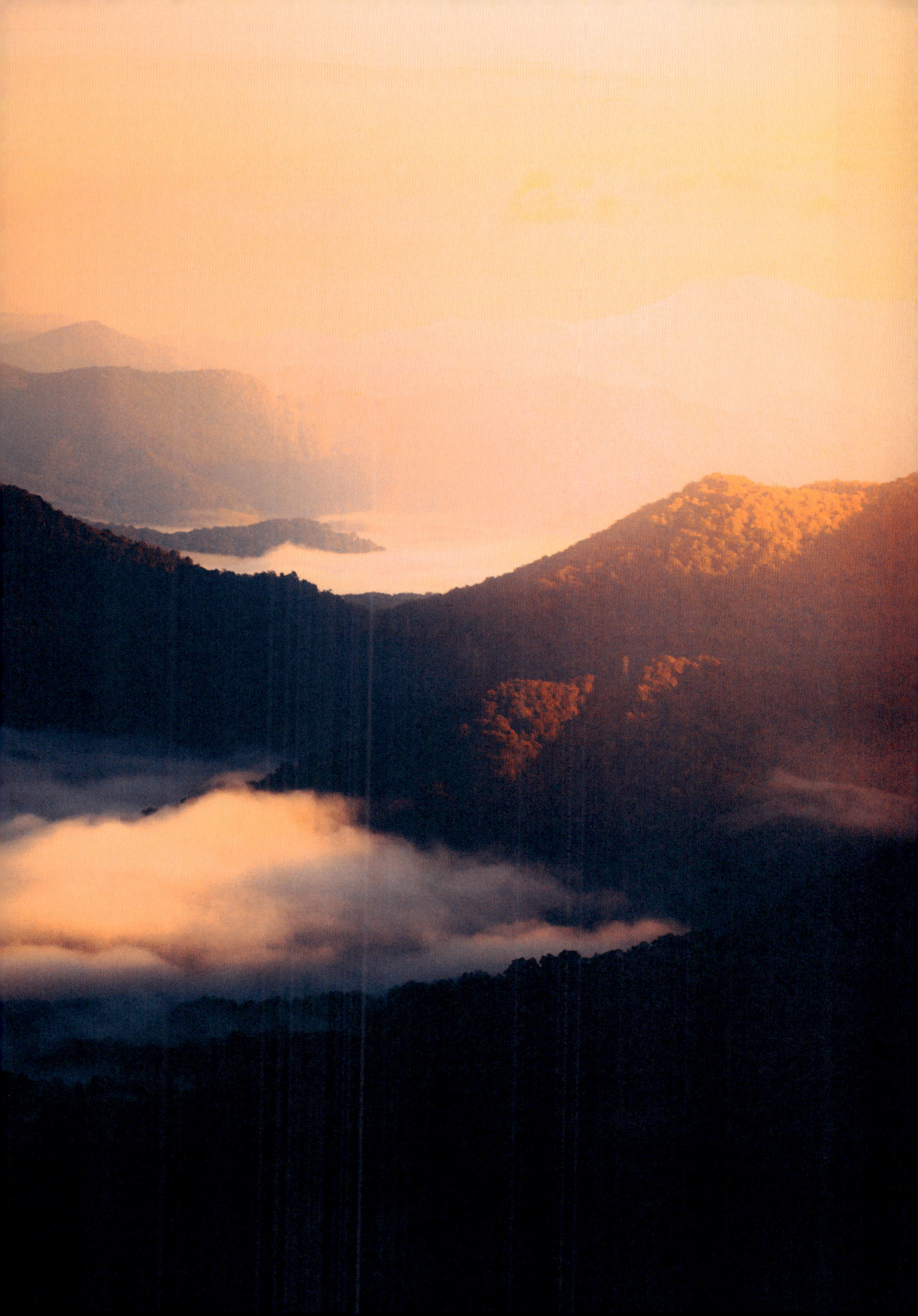

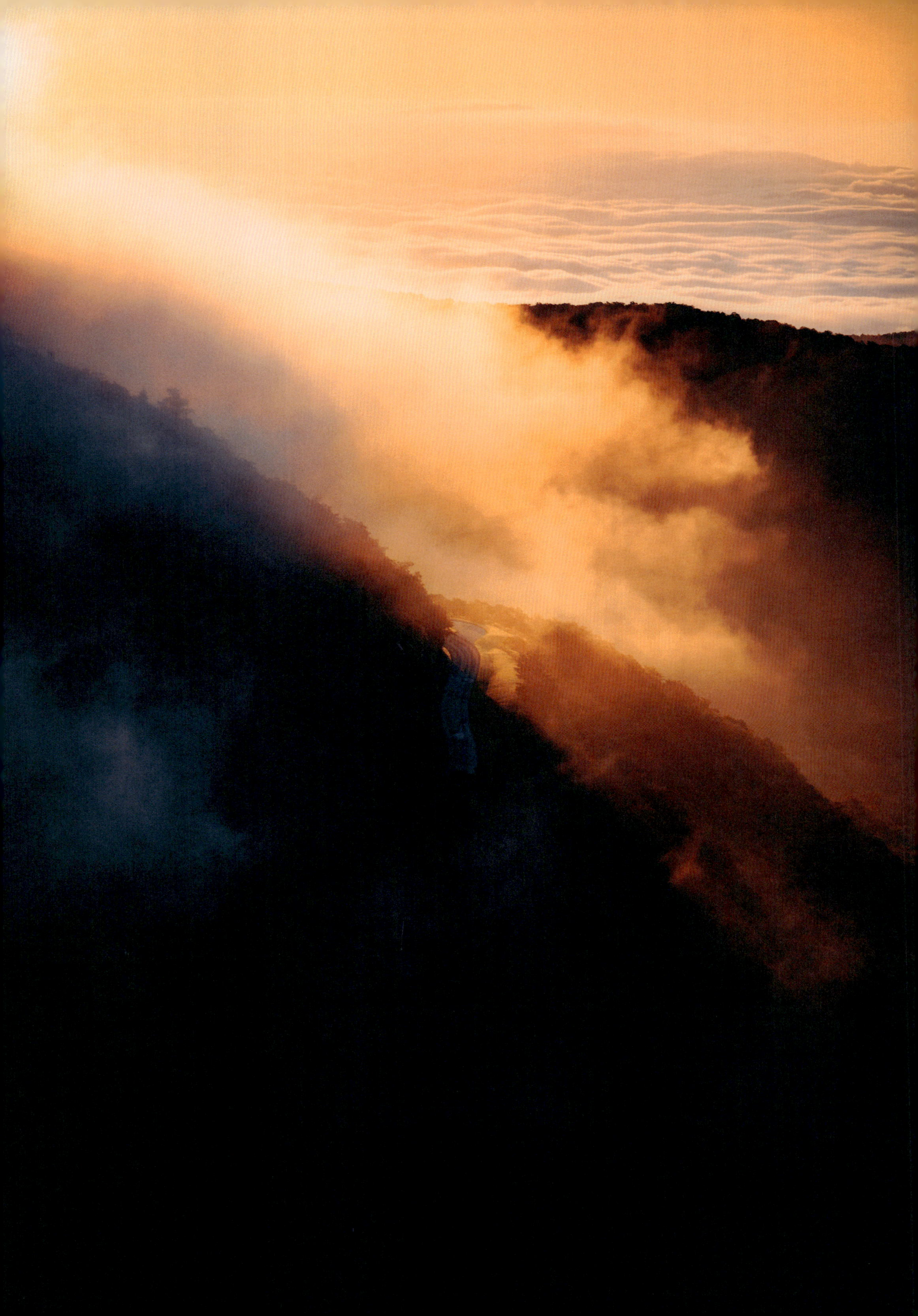

The Mountains Are a Lonely Folk

The mountains they are silent folk
    They stand afar – alone,
And the clouds that kiss their brows at night
Hear neither sigh nor groan.
    Each bears him in his ordered place
As soldiers do, and bold and high
They fold their forests round their feet
And bolster up the sky.

HAMLIN GARLAND

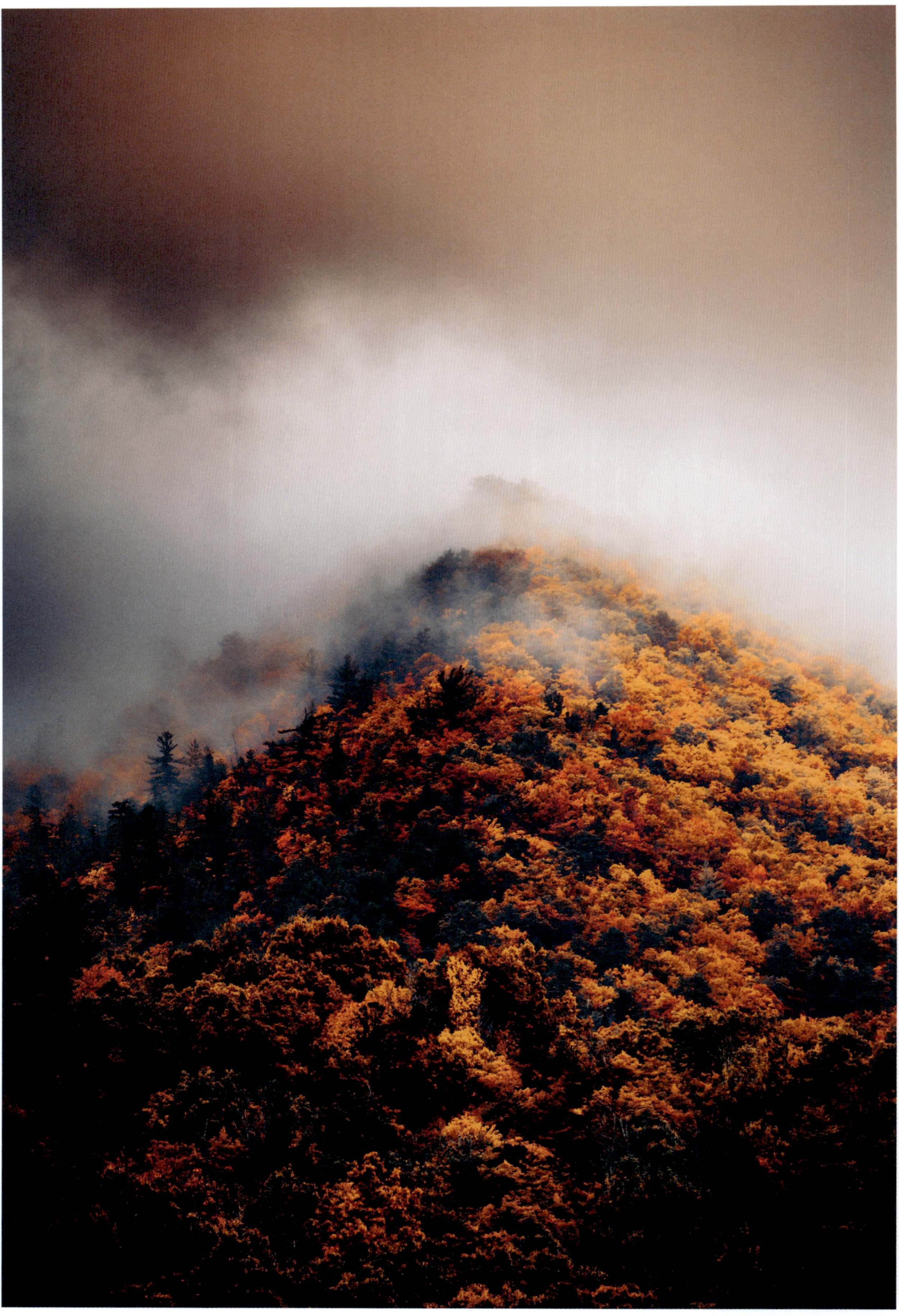

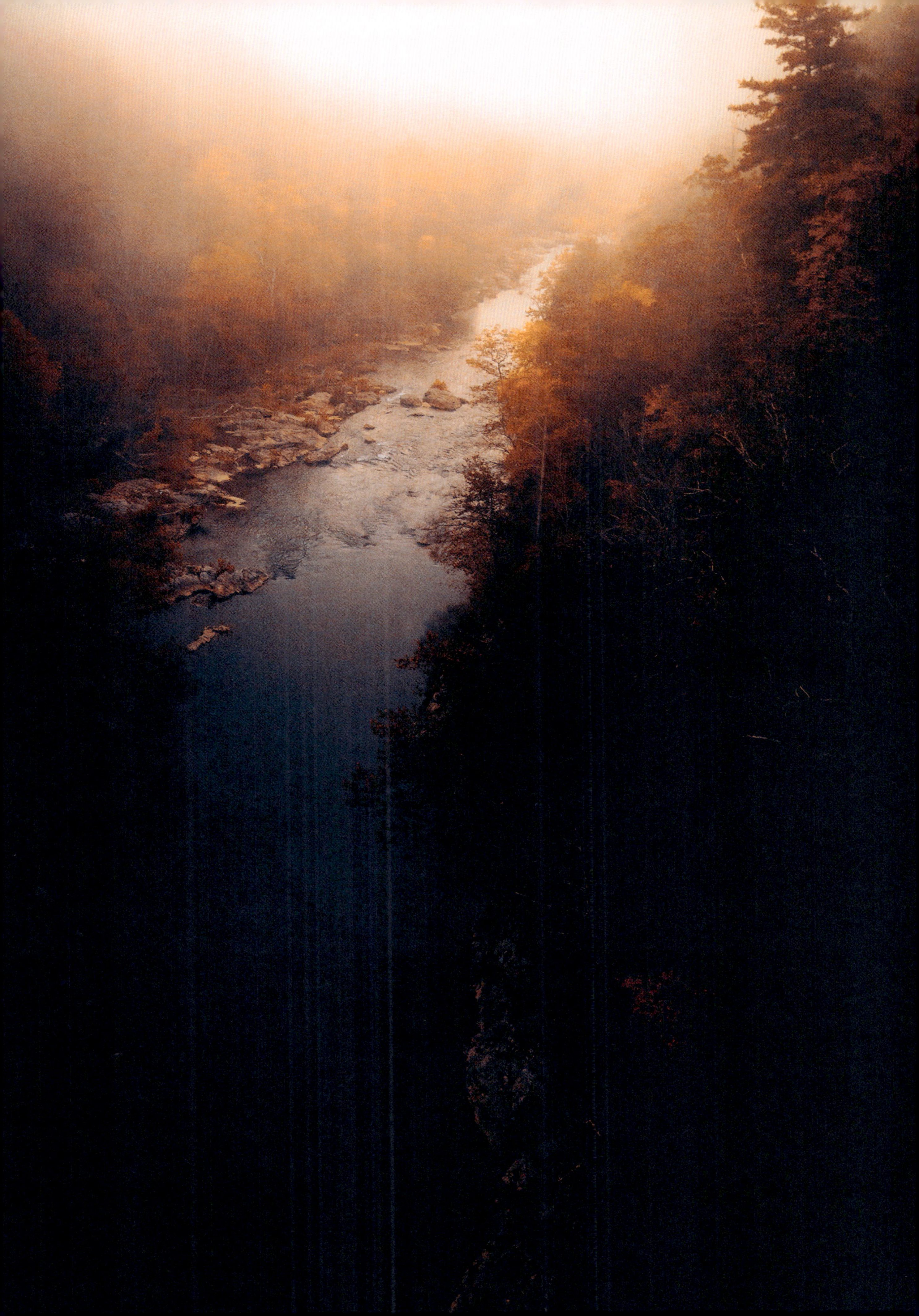

The Laurel

The mountain laurel is rosy cloud-drifts

Over the wood's brown floor

Cumulous masses,

Rounded,

Tipped with crimson,

Foam up from the dark green leaves.

More and more,

Like the sweep of bright spoil over the blue

When the storm has gone,

They move over and under

The sunshine and shadow,

Capturing the new-blown Summer

As she walks in the wood.

HARRIET MONROE

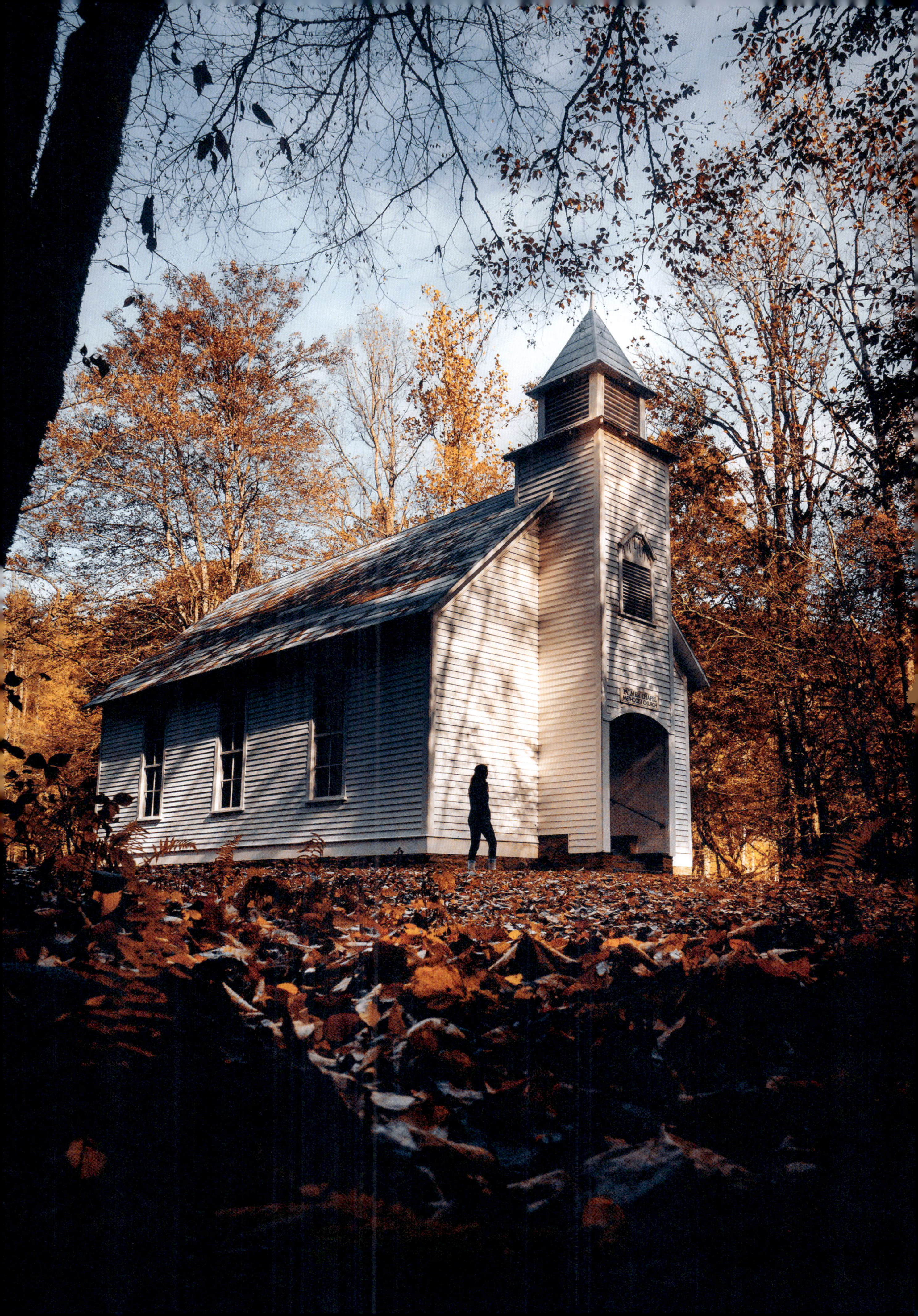
PALMER CHAPEL
METHODIST CHURCH

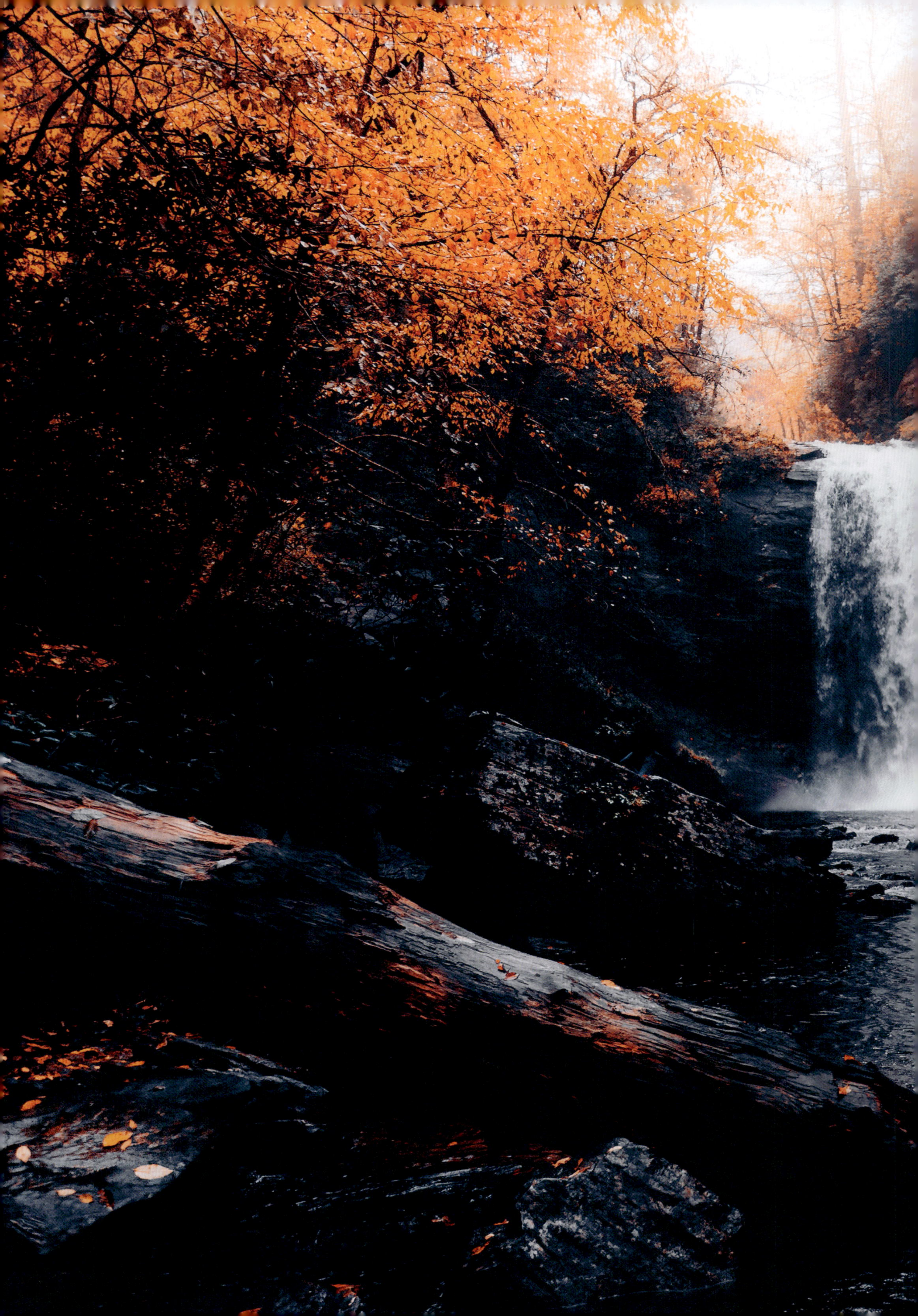

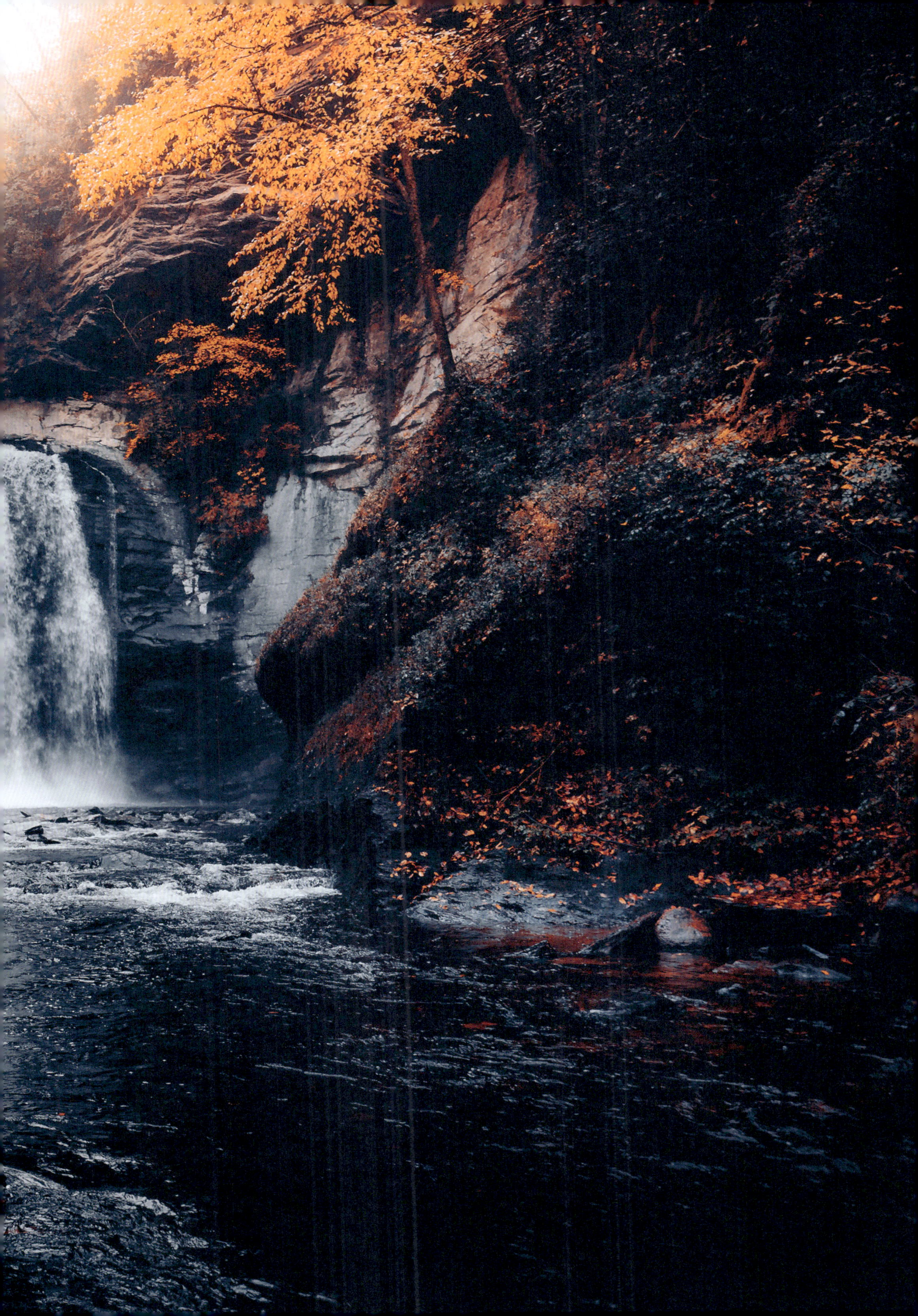

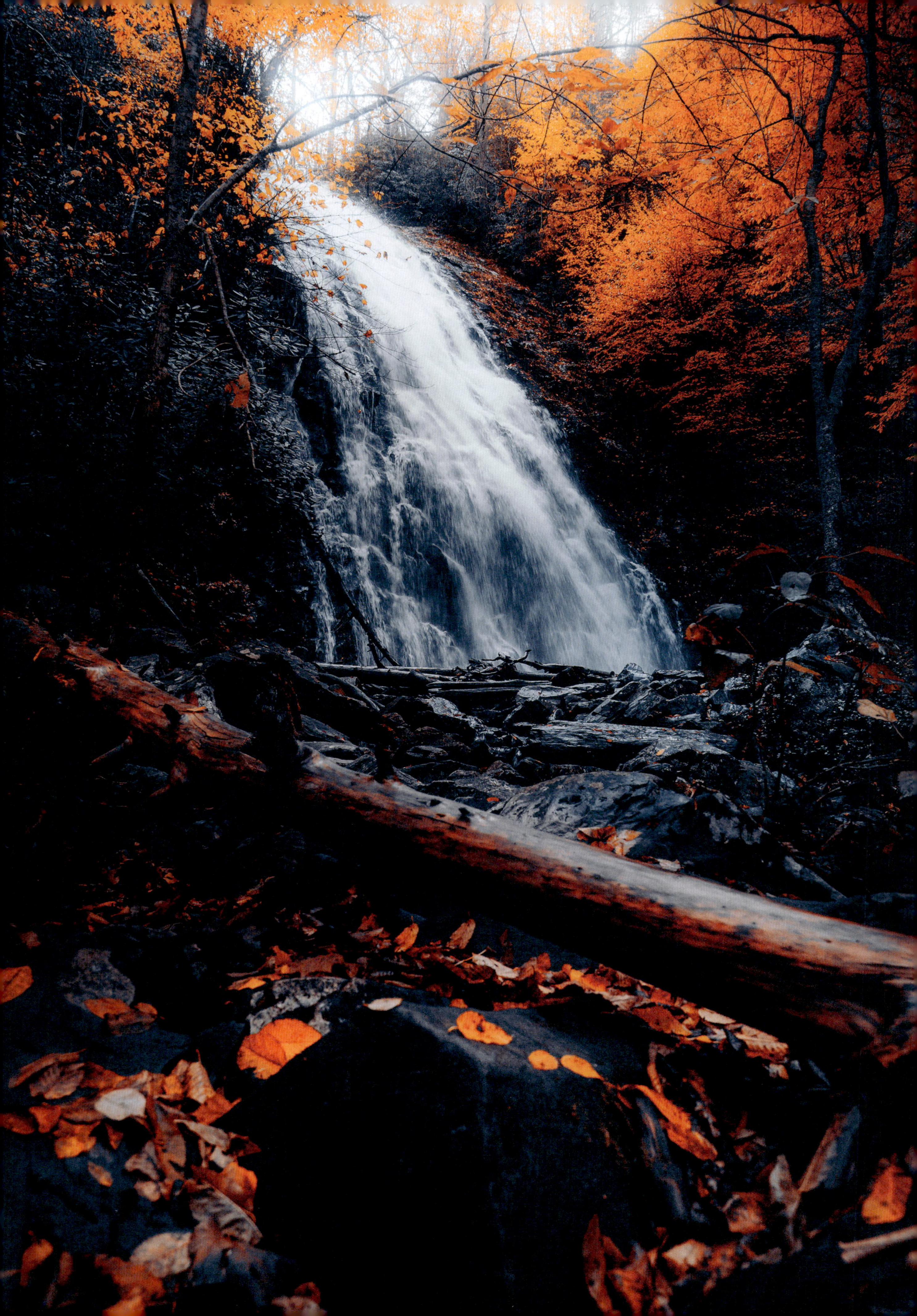

Running Water

Yes, I move, I live, I wander astray –
     Water running, intermingling, over the sands.
I know the passionate pleasure of motion;
     I taste the forests; I touch strange lands.

Yes, I move – perhaps I am seeking
     Storms, suns, dawns, a place to hide.
What are you doing here, pale and polished –
     You, the stone in the path of the tide?

ALFONSINA STORNI

A true conservationist
is a man who knows
that the world is not
given by his fathers,
but borrowed from
his children.

JOHN JAMES AUDUBON

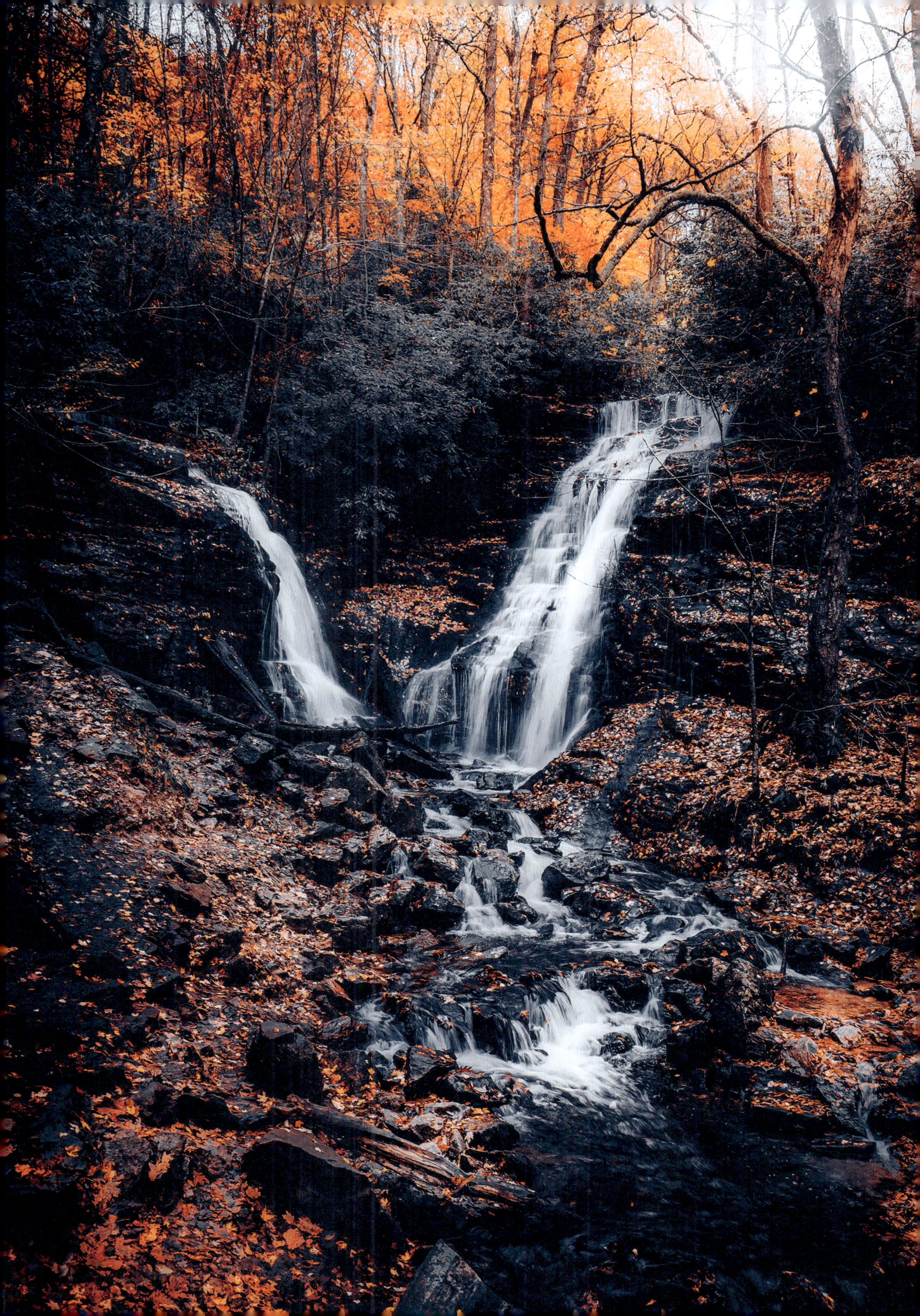

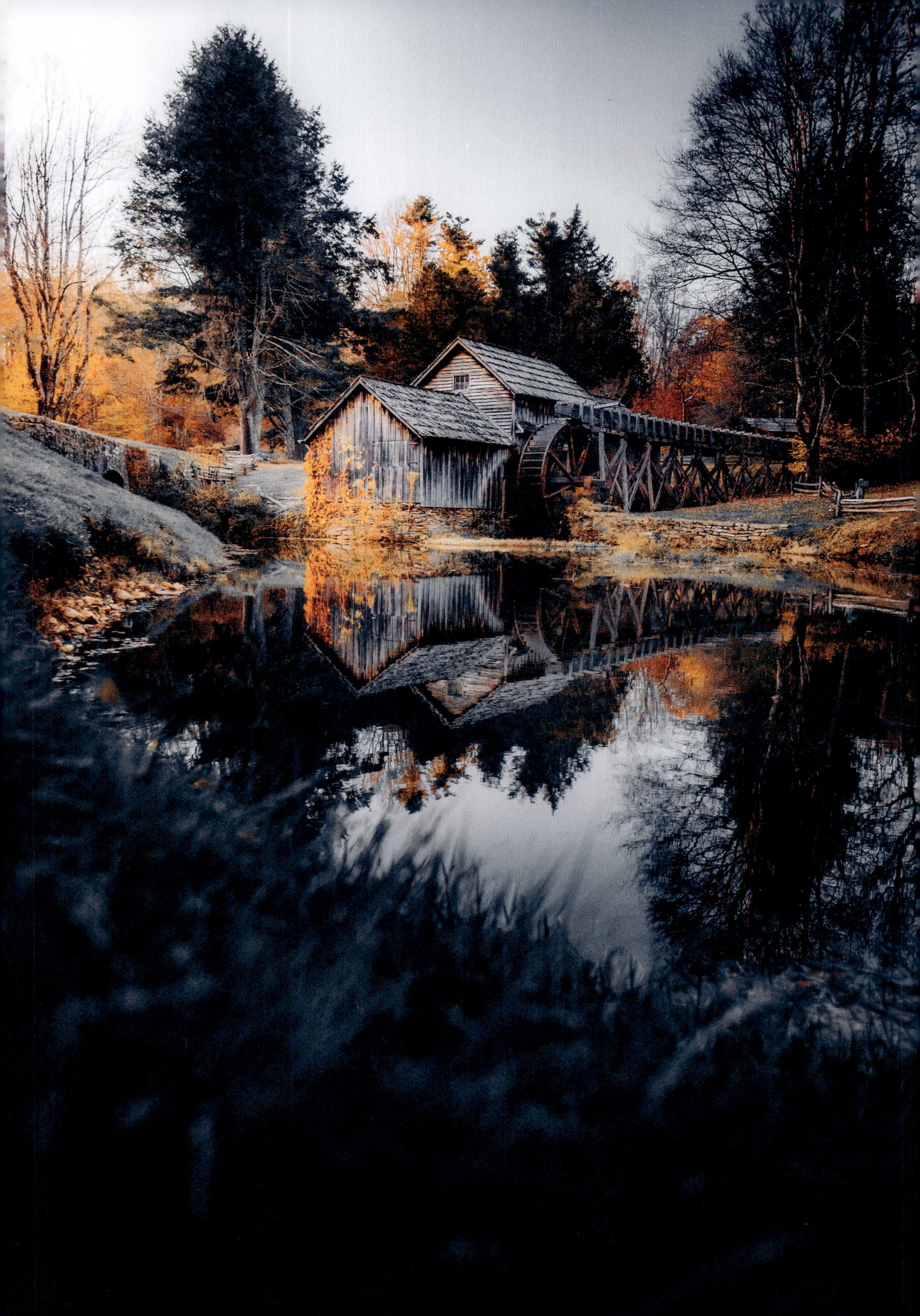

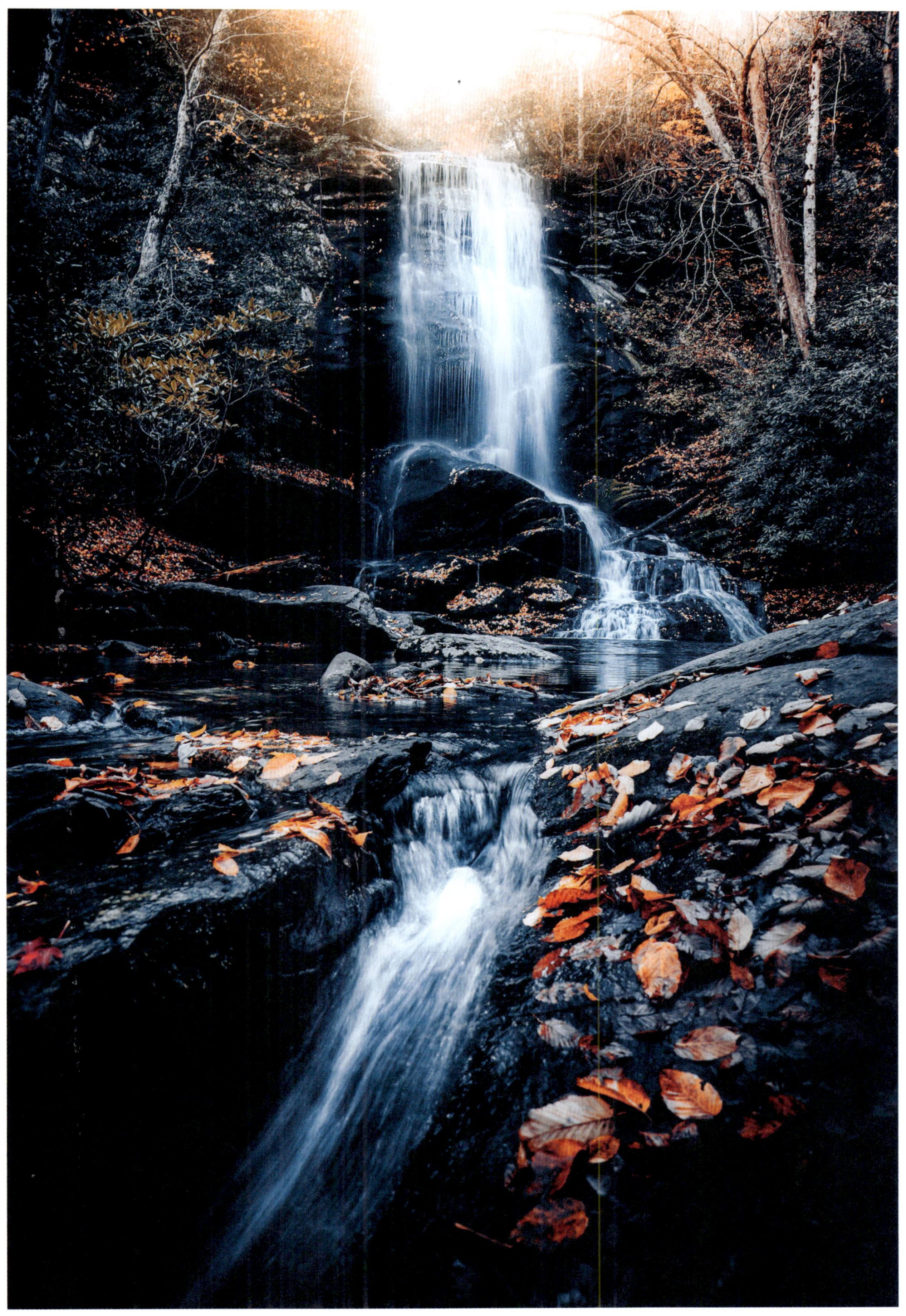

Although we say
mountains belong
to the country,
actually, they
belong to those
that love them.

DŌGEN

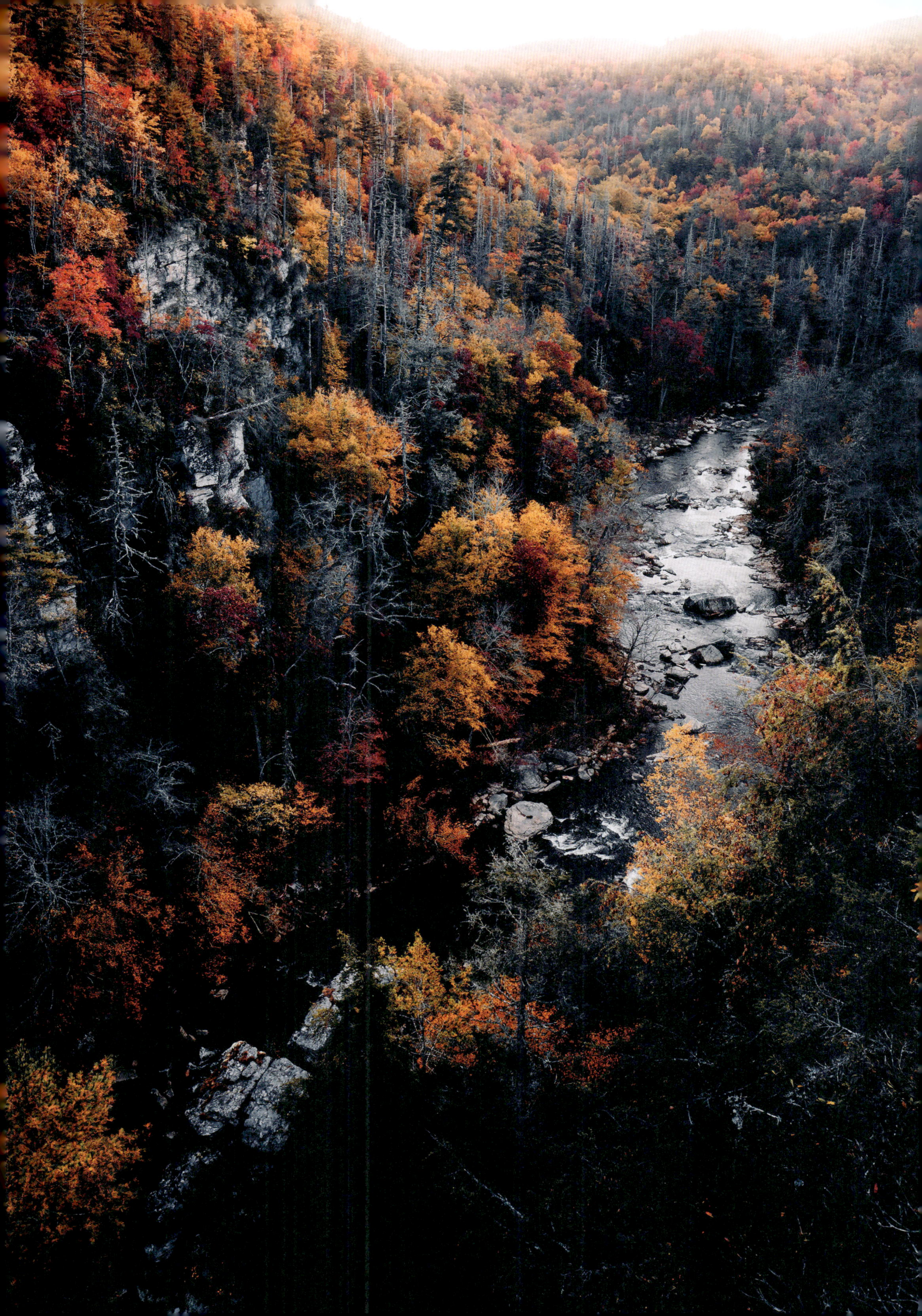

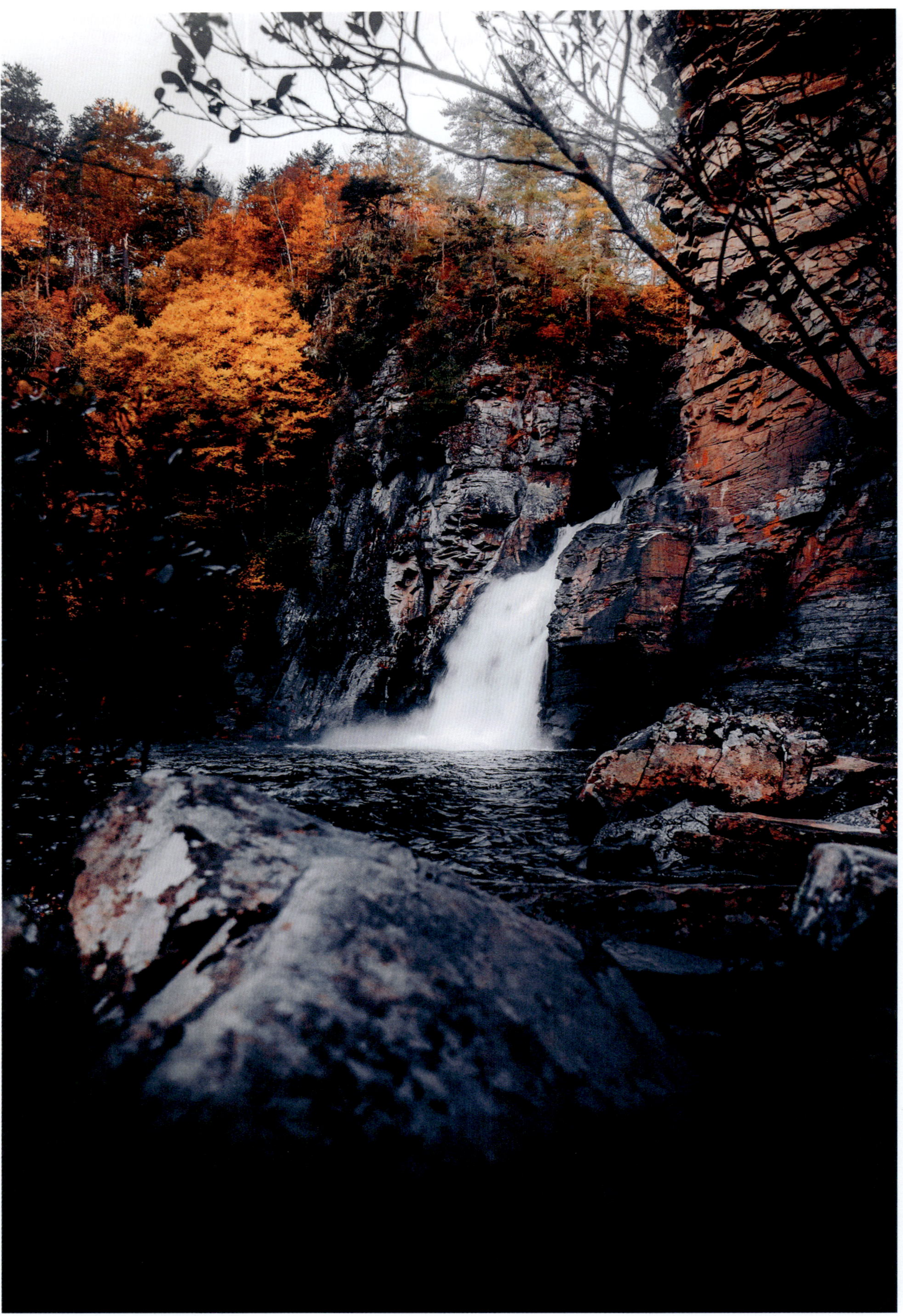

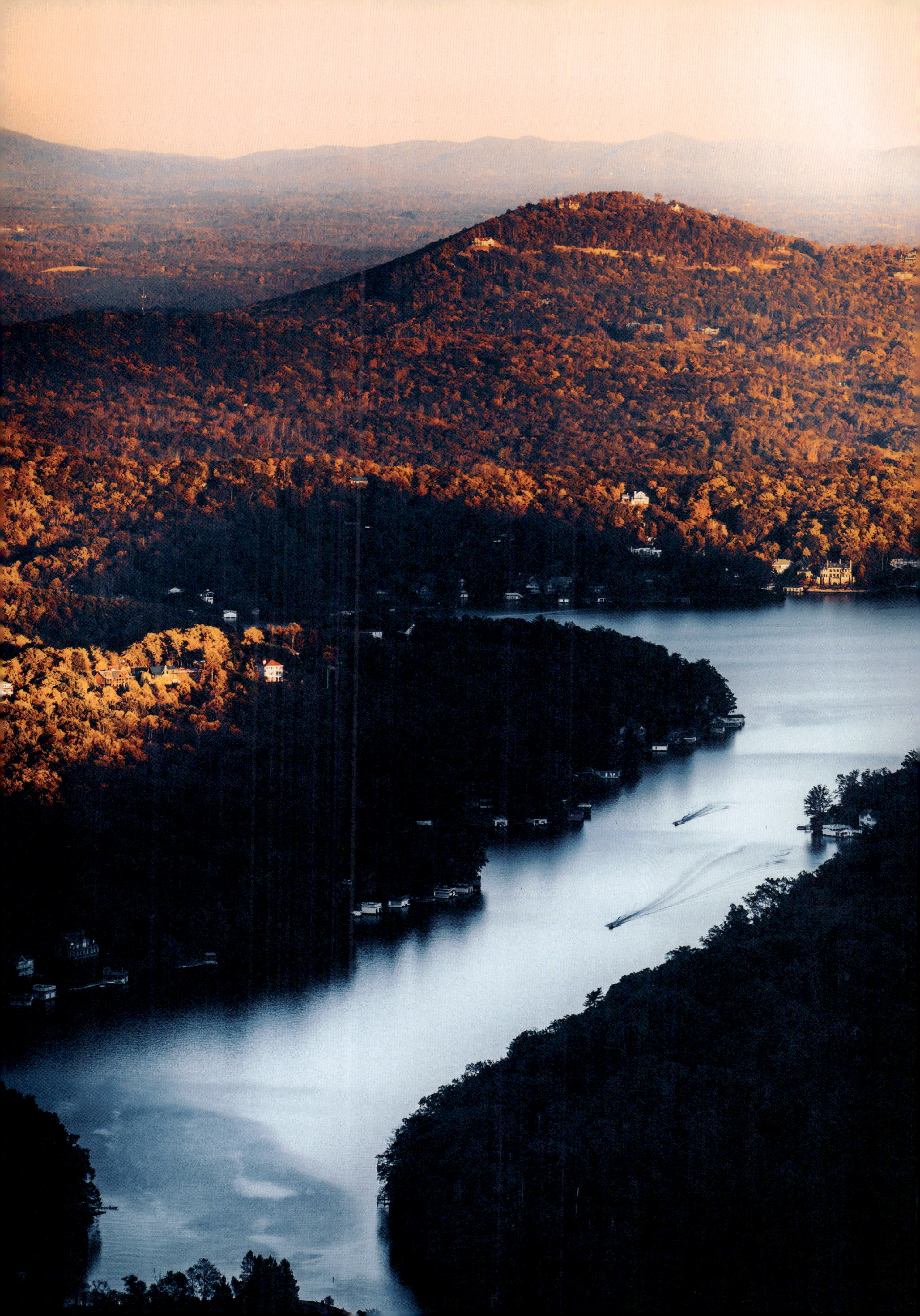

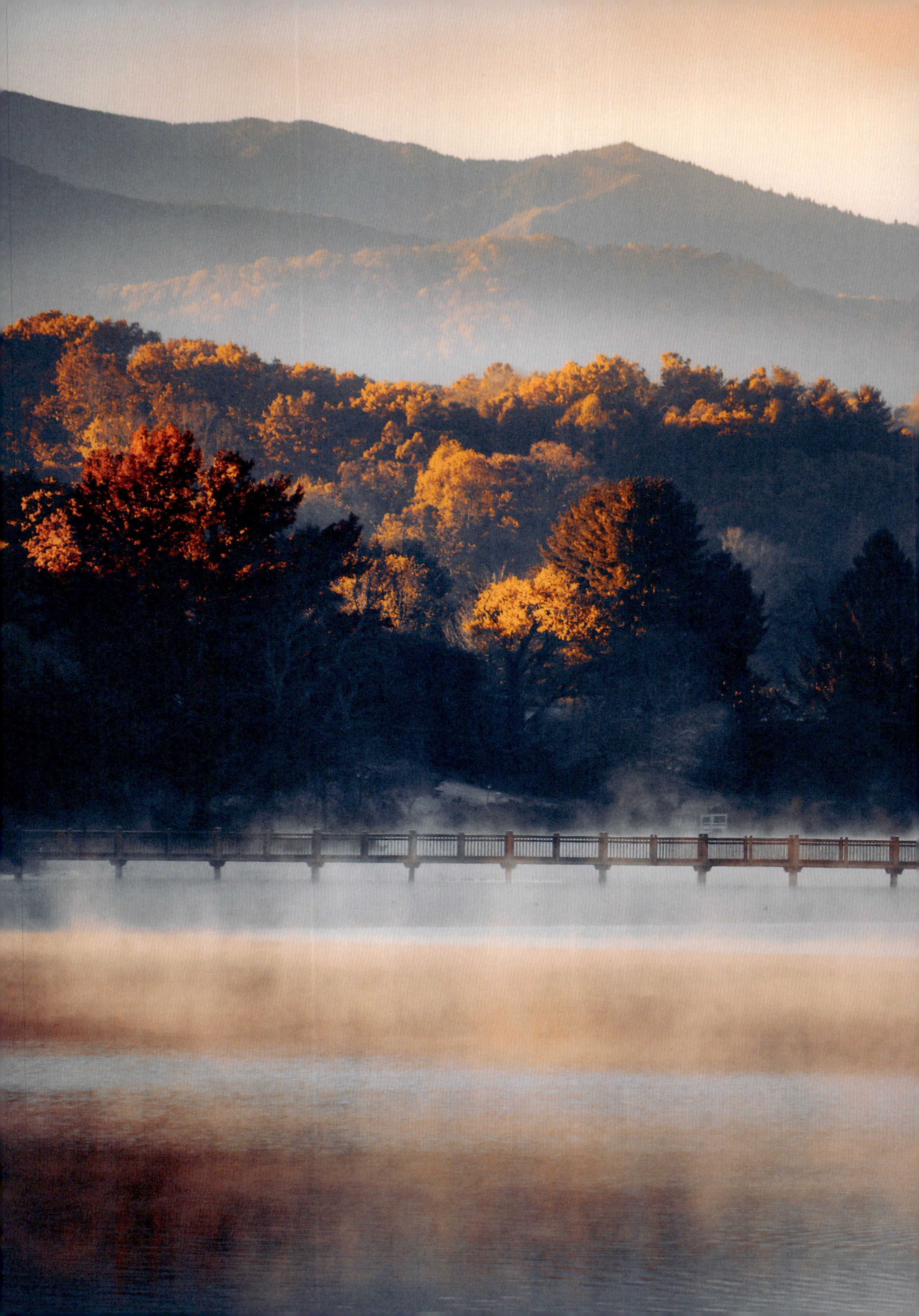

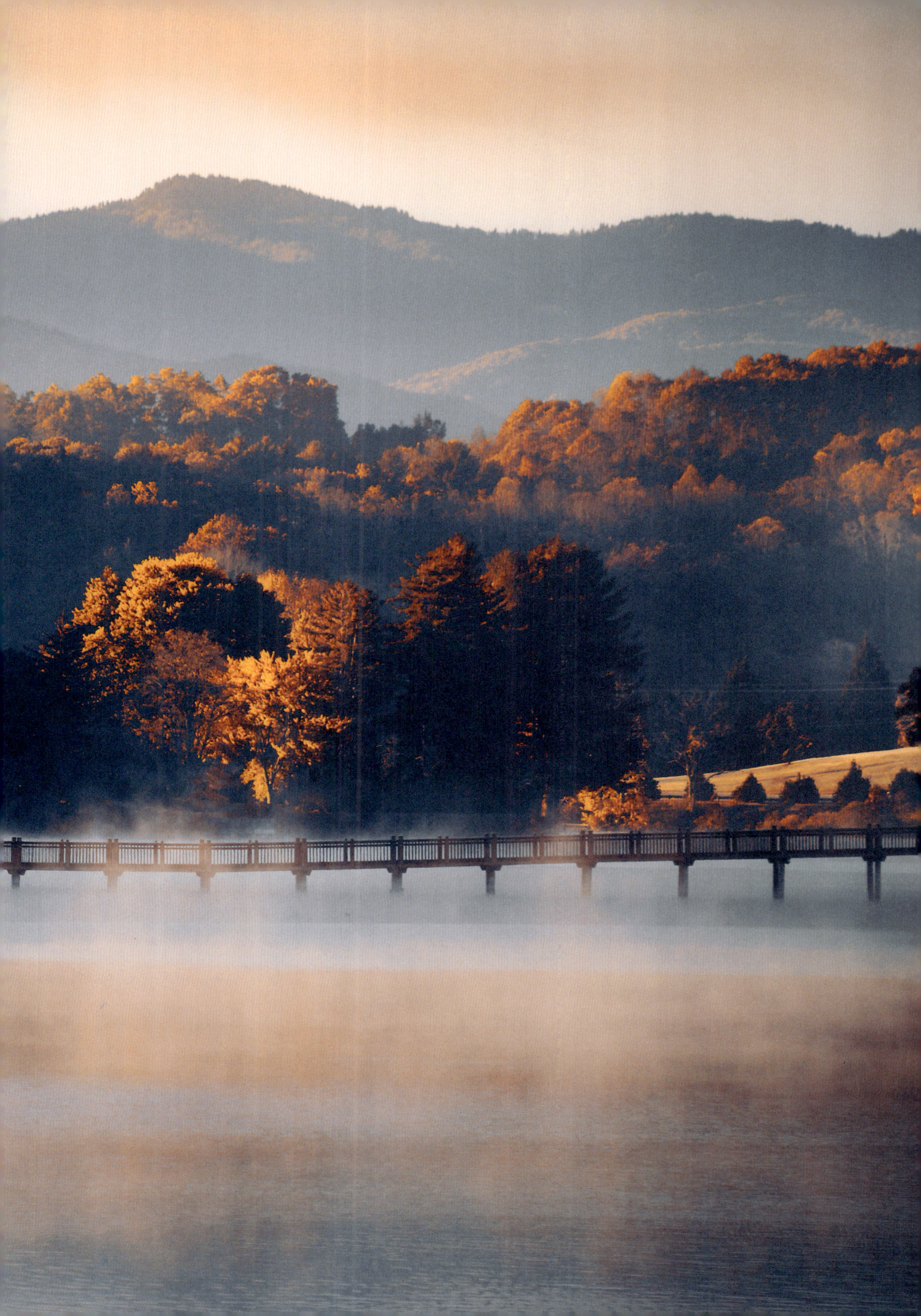

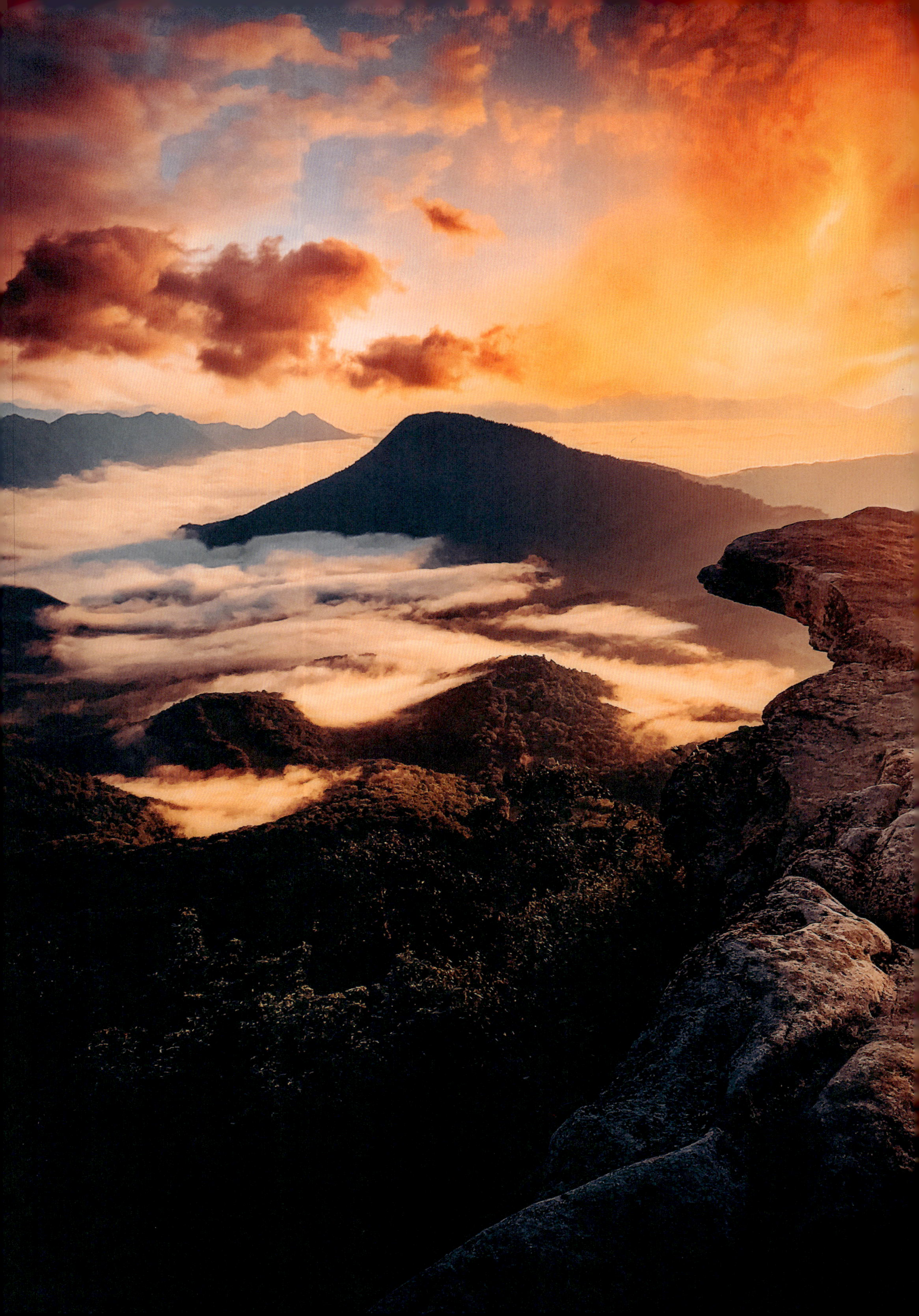

MIKE POGGIOLI

Originally from just outside New York City, Mike Poggioli came to see
photography as a serious creative outlet when he moved to Chicago in
2015 and became enamored by the beauty of the city's architecture.
He then brought his newfound love for cityscapes with him to Cincinnati,
Ohio, where he studied clinical psychology. Photography became an
opportunity to cultivate mindfulness – a way to see the world with a
beginner's mind – in both his personal life and professional practice.
It wasn't until he began a clinical internship in Asheville, North Carolina,
that he ventured into landscape photography. During his time there, Mike
discovered a passion for capturing the layers of the Blue Ridge Mountains.
He has since listened to the call of the mountains by deciding to settle
in Asheville.

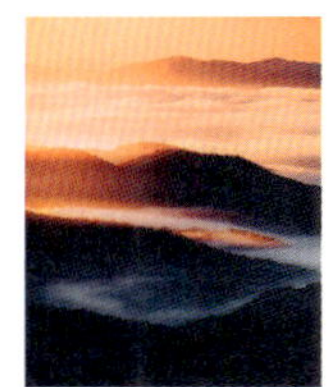

2 Blue Ridge Parkway, Looking Glass Rock Overlook, NC

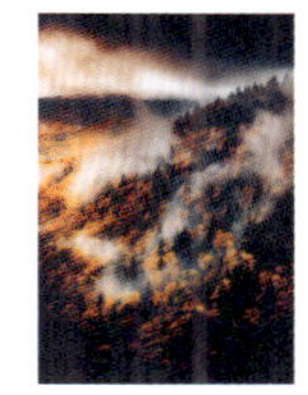

4 Blue Ridge Parkway, Herrin Knob Overlook, NC

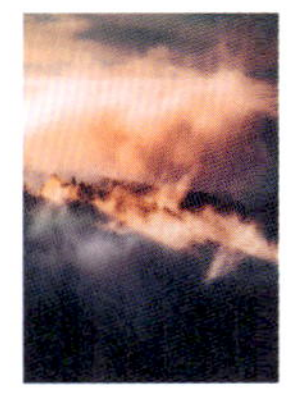

7 Waterrock Knob Visitor Center, NC

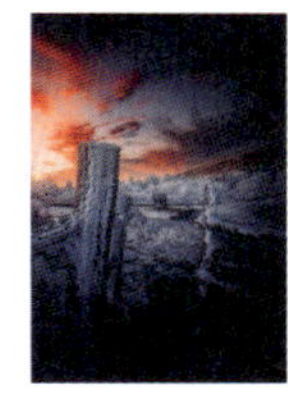

8 Carver's Gap, NC/TN

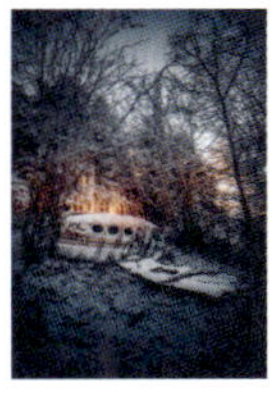

9 Waterrock Knob, NC

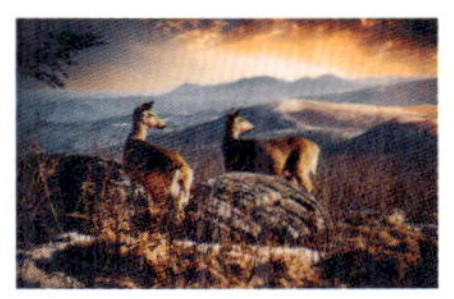

10-11 Grassy Ridge Bald, NC/TN

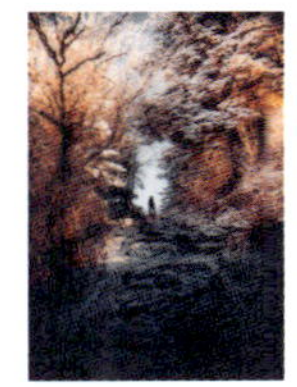

13 Waterrock Kncb, NC

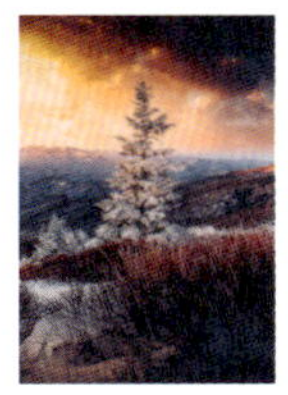

14 Roan Mountain, NC/TN

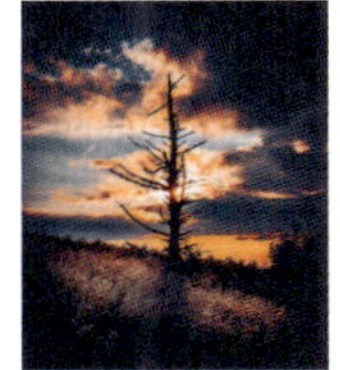

15 Round Bald, NC/TN

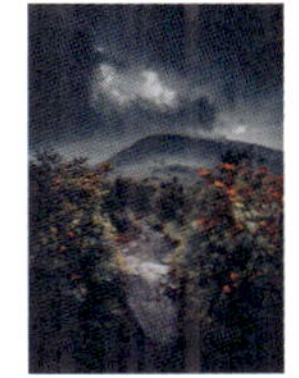

16 Jane Bald, NC/TN

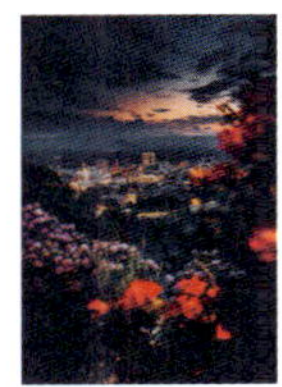

17 Asheville, NC

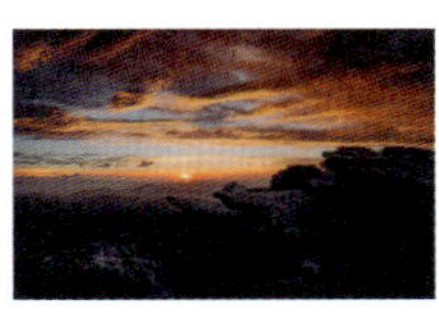

18-19 Hawksbill Mountain, NC

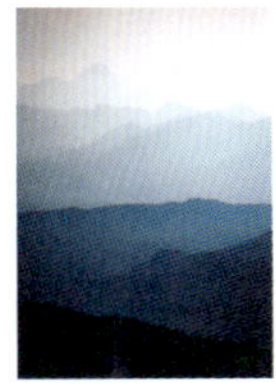

21 View from McAfee Knob, VA

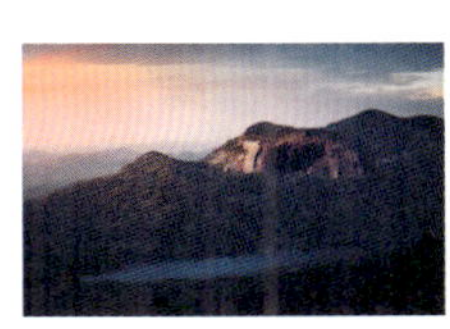

22-23 Table Rock from Caesars Head Overlook, SC

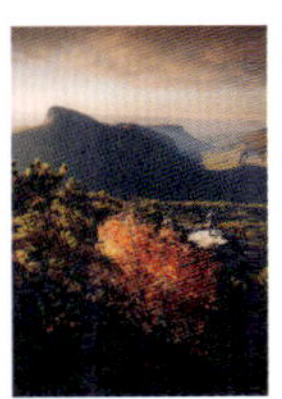

24 Hawksbill Mountain, Linville Gorge, NC

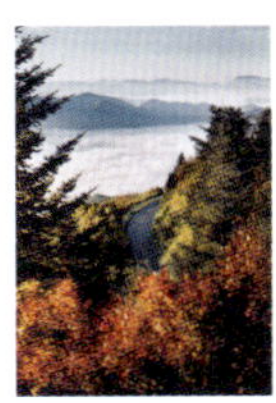

25 Waterrock Knob Visitor Center, NC/TN

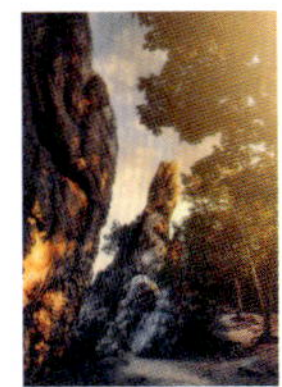

26 Dragon's Tooth, VA

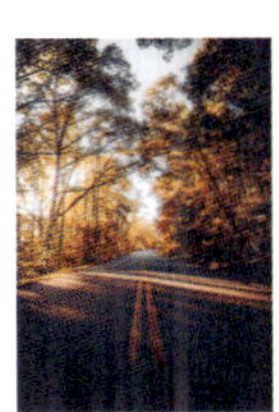

27 Blue Ridge Parkway, Near Haw Creek Valley Overlook, NC

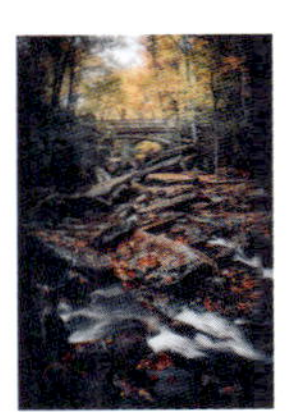

29 Wilson Creek Eridge, Tanawah Trail, NC

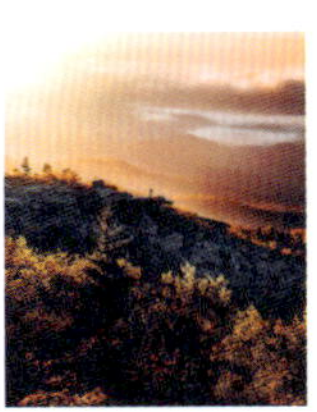

30 Rough Ridge, NC

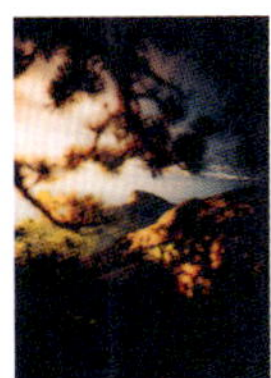

31 Table Rock, Linville Gorge, NC

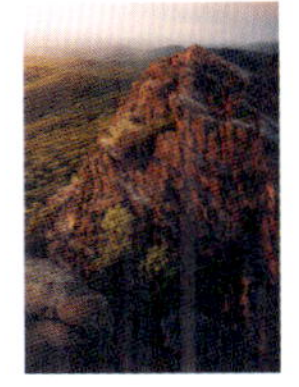

32 Humpback Rock, VA

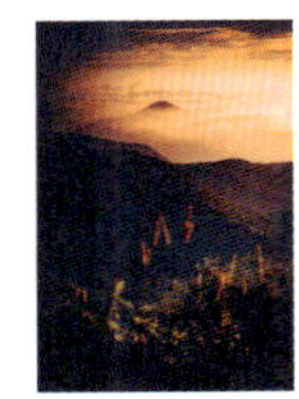

33 Mt. Pisgah f-om Black Balsam Knob, NC

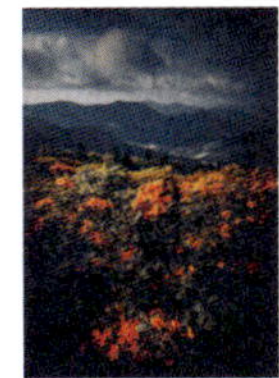

35 Round Bald, NC/TN

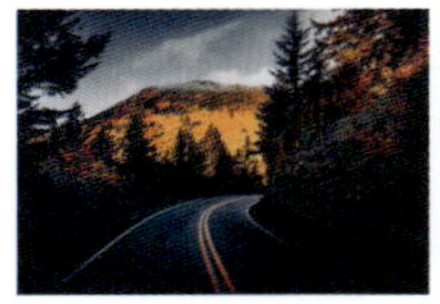

36-37 Mt. Mitchell, NC

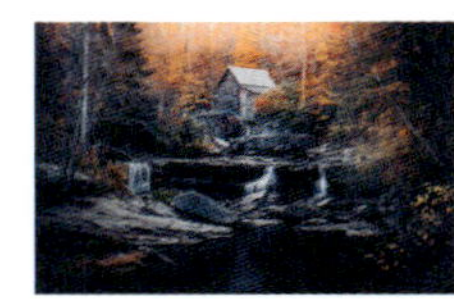

38-39 Glade Creek Grist Mill, Babcock State Park, WV

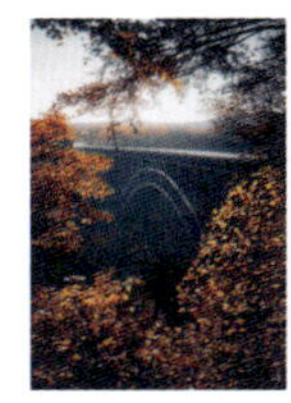

40 New River Gorge Bridge, WV

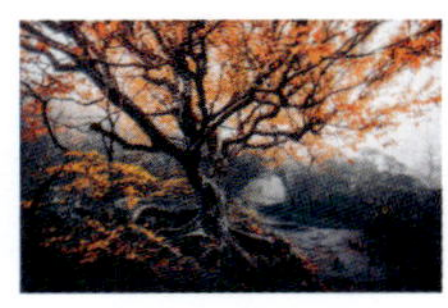

42-43 Craggy Gardens, NC

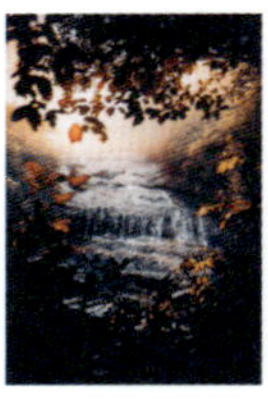

44 Graveyard Fields, Lower Falls, NC

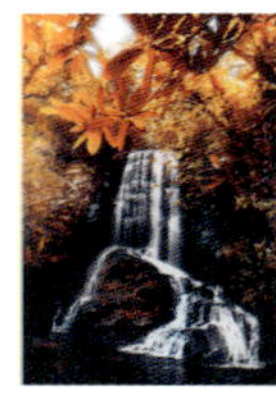

45 Upper Catawba Falls, NC

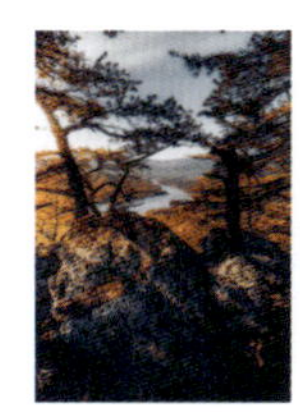

46 Appalachian Trail Near Hay Rock, VA

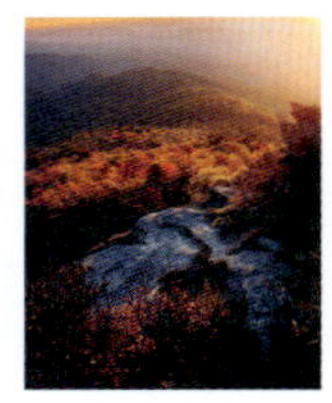

48 Hawksbill Mountain, NC

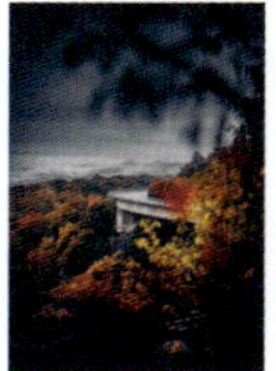

49 Blue Ridge Parkway, Linn Cove Viaduct, NC

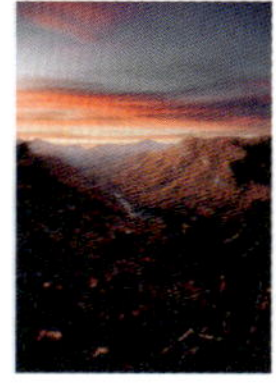

50 Chimney Rock State Park, NC

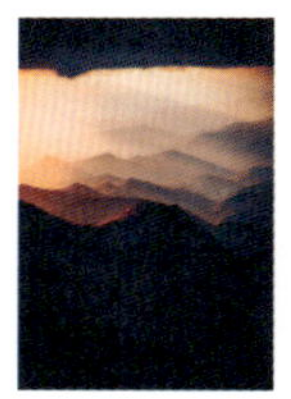

51 Blue Ridge Parkway, Woolyback Overlook, NC

52 Waterrock Knob Visitor Center, NC

54-55 View from Mt. Mitchell, NC

57 Looking Glass Rock, NC

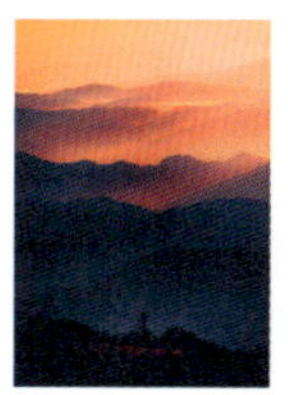

58 Round Bald, NC/TN

59 Blue Ridge Parkway, Mills River Valley Overlook, NC

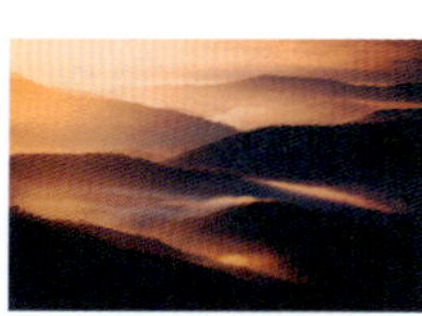

60-61 Blue Ridge Parkway, Mills River Valley Overlook, NC

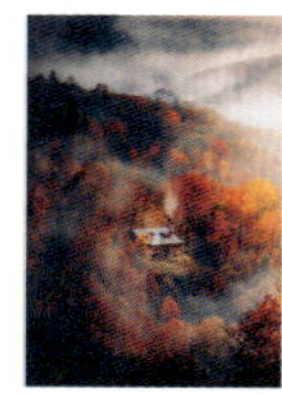

62 Blue Ridge Parkway, Crabtree Falls, NC

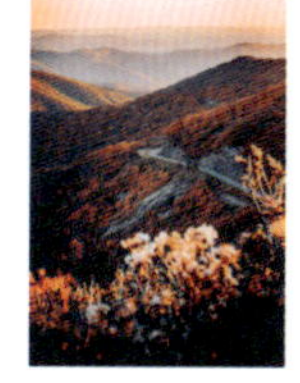

64 Craggy Dome Overlook, NC

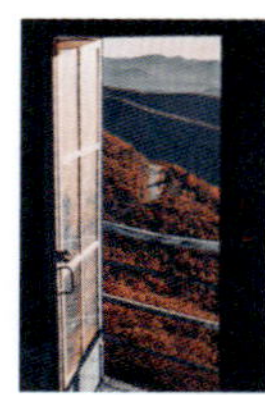

65 Fryingpan Mountain Lookout Tower, NC

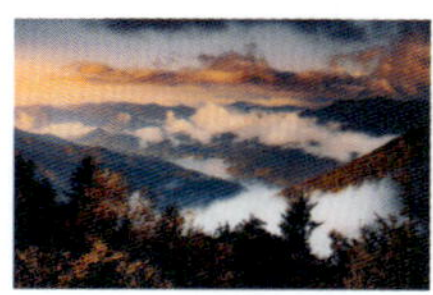

66-67 Blue Ridge Parkway, Burnett Reservoir, NC

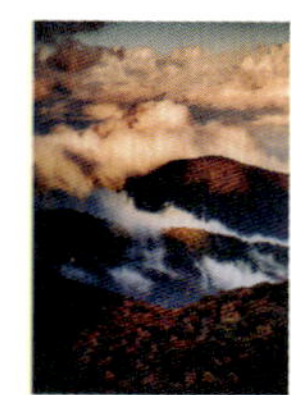

68 Blue Ridge Parkway, East Fork Overlook, NC

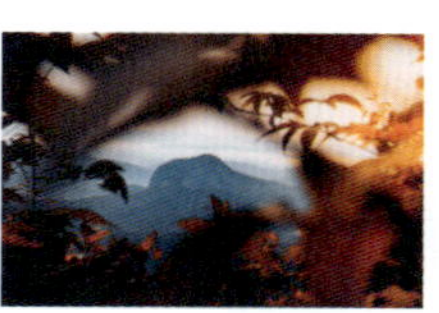

70-71 Looking Glass Rock, NC

72 Blue Ridge Parkway, Pounding Mill Overlook, NC

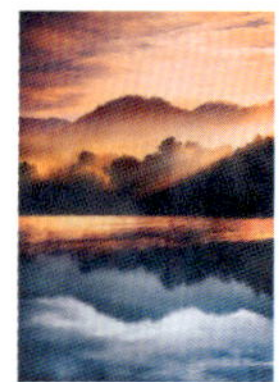

73 Beaver Lake, NC

74 Hawksbill Mountain, NC

76–77 Blue Ridge Parkway, Mills River Overlook, NC

78–79 Blue Ridge Parkway, Pounding Mill Overlook, NC

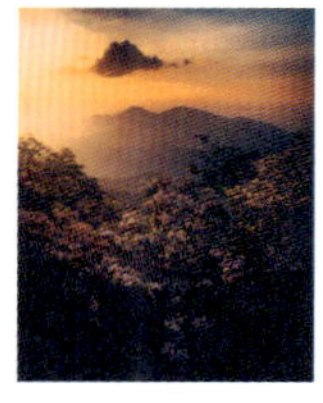

80 Blue Ridge Parkway, Green Knob Overlook, NC

82–83 Fryingpan Mountain Lookout Tower, NC

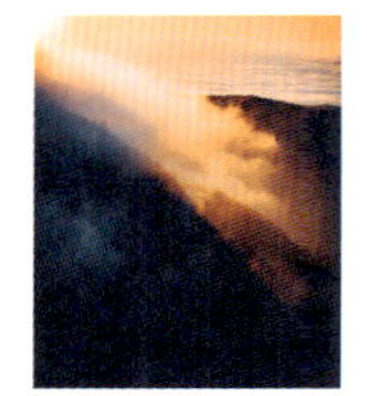

84 Fryingpan Mountain Lookout Tower, NC

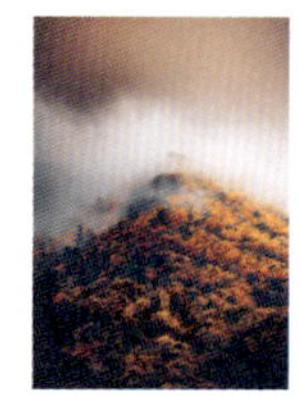

86 Cataloochee Valley, TN

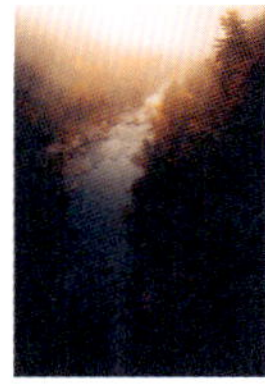

87 Blue Ridge Parkway, Roanoke River Overlook, VA

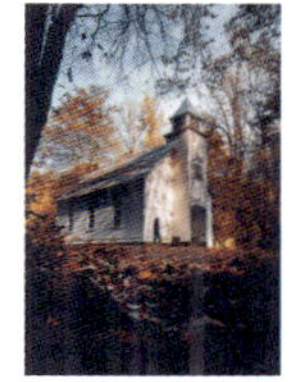

89 Palmer Chapel, Cataloochee Valley, TN

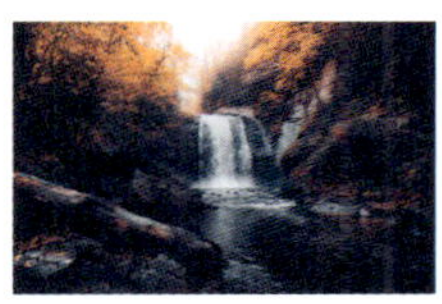

90–91 Looking Glass Falls, NC

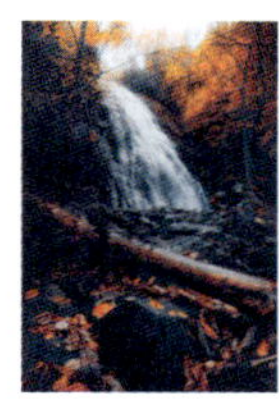

92 Crabtree Falls, NC

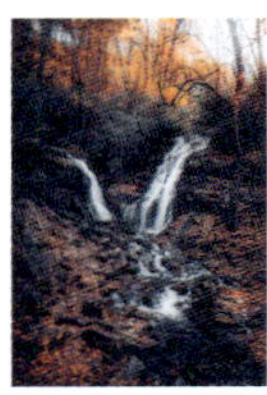

95 Soco Falls, NC

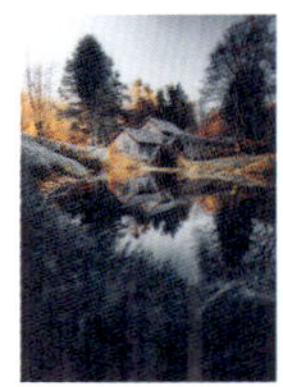

96 Mabry Mill, VA

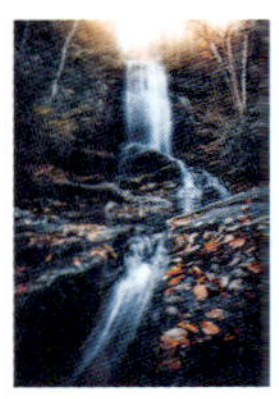

97 Upper Catawba Falls, NC

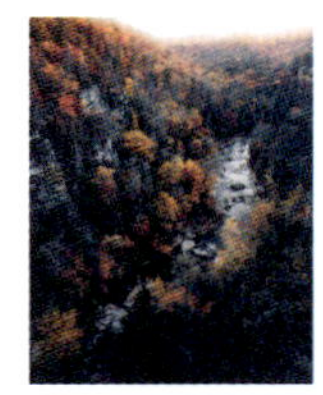

99 Linville Falls, NC

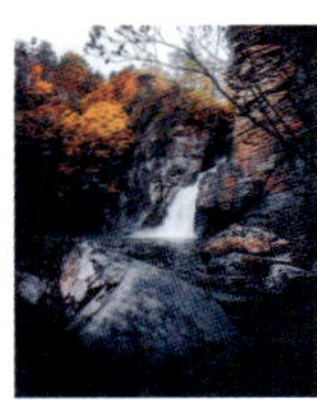

100 Linville Falls, NC

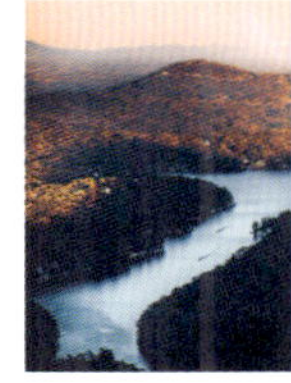

101 View of Lake Lure from Chimney Rock, NC

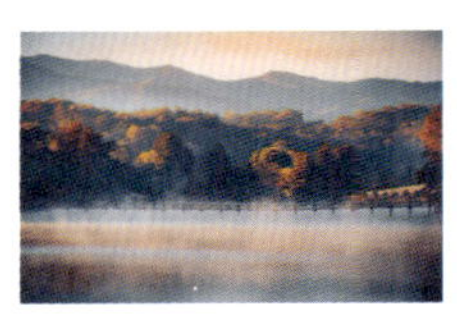

102–103 Lake Junaluska, NC

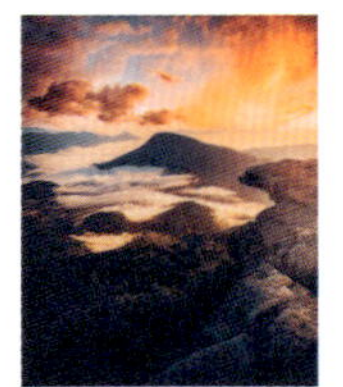

104 McAfee Knob, VA

111 View of the Smokies from Waterrock Knob, NC

LCCN: 2022939947
ISBN: 978-1-951963-12-5

Printed and bound in China
Third printing, 2025

Trope Publishing Co.

All poems reprinted with permission as required.

Mike Poggioli's photographs are available
for purchase. For inquires, go to trope.com
or email the gallery at info@trope.com

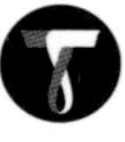

+ INFORMATION:
For additional information
on our books and prints,
visit trope.com

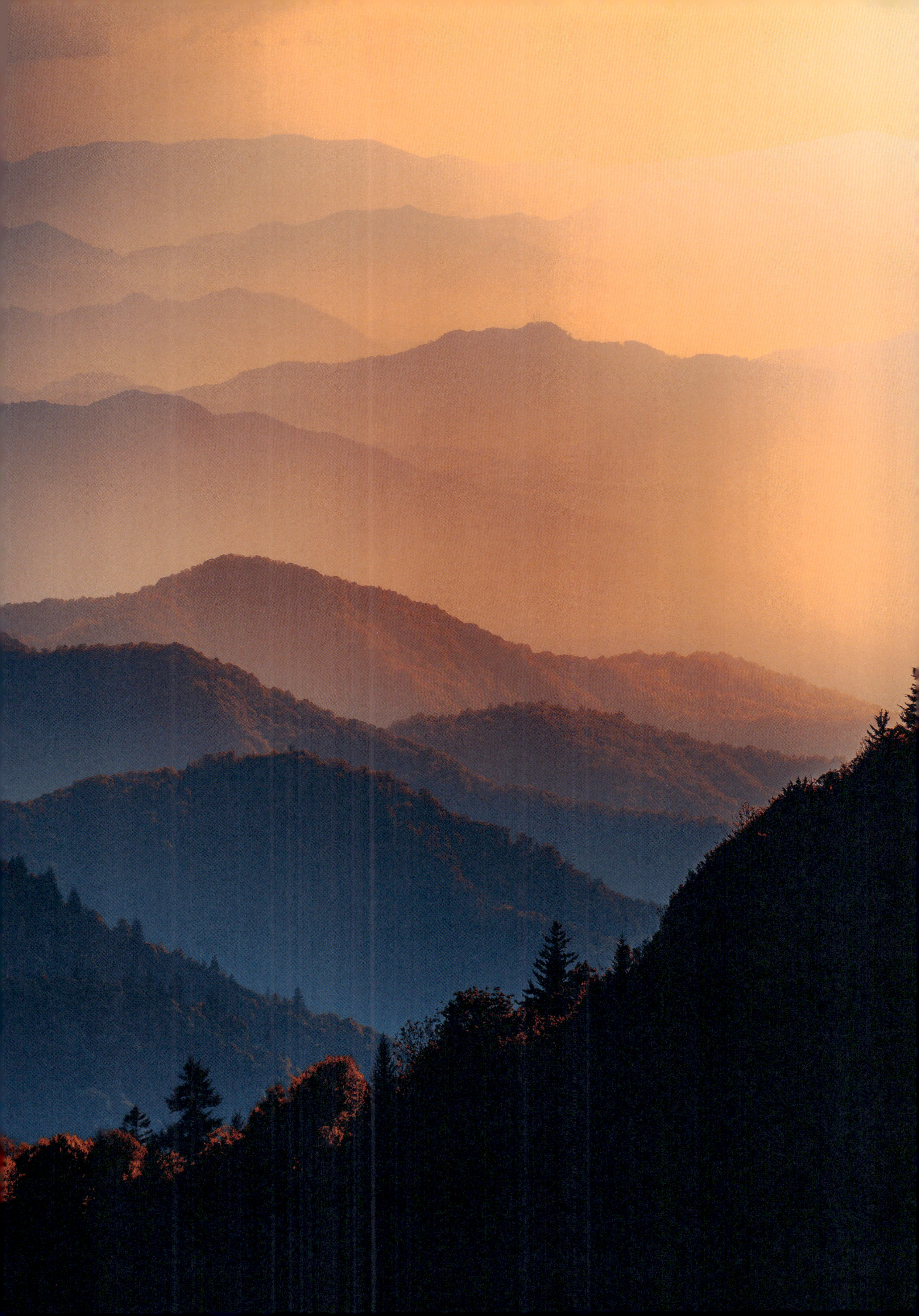

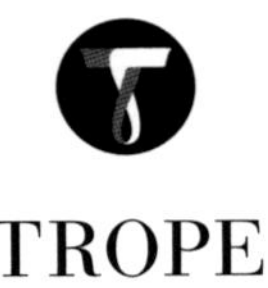

TROPE

TROPE PUBLISHING Co.